N. 2021

To Phoebe,

fight the good .

Brené

THE NEW CIVIL WAR

The New Civil War: Exposing Elites, Fighting Utopian Leftism, and Restoring America

For more information, please contact:
Amplify Publishing, an imprint of Mascot Books
620 Herndon Parkway, Suite 320
Herndon, VA 20170
info@mascotbooks.com

Library of Congress Control Number: 2021902543
CPSIA Code: PRV0321A
ISBN-13: 978-1-64543-840-3

Printed in the United States

To my children and their entire generation,
for whose sake we must restore America.

FOREWORD BY SEBASTIAN GORKA, PhD
FORMER STRATEGIST TO PRESIDENT TRUMP

BRUCE D. ABRAMSON

THE NEW CIVIL WAR

EXPOSING ELITES

FIGHTING PROGRESSIVISM

AND RESTORING AMERICA

CONTENTS

FOREWORD

Restoration or revolution? That is the stark choice Bruce Abramson lays before us in *The New Civil War*, and for me this is an especially intimate question. Why? Because I would not be living as a free man in the greatest nation on Earth were it not for an actual revolution.

As the child of parents who escaped a communist dictatorship during the momentous events of the Hungarian Revolution, my father liberated from a political prison by a band of freedom fighters who had captured a Soviet tank, I never would have been born were it not for those who chose to fight for liberty.

After the events of November 2020, are Americans condemned to the same fate: to fight a bloody revolution? I dearly hope not, given that the deadliest war we ever fought was the one in which Americans slew Americans. The two World Wars, Korea, and Vietnam took fewer lives in toto than the four years of our own Civil War. God preserve us from another such bloodbath.

But something has to be done. Those that love the republic know that the 2020 election was a travesty—without reading even one of the thousands of sworn affidavits or examining the forensic evidence. All else aside, we are now expected to believe that a cognitively challenged old man, a machine politician for forty-seven years, ensconced in his basement for months, venturing out infrequently to host "rallies" with attendance in double digits, received more votes than either of his two immediate predecessors: America's first-ever black president and a commander-in-chief who could fill a stadium with twenty-five thousand screaming supporters, week after week, often day after day?

Americans are in part defined by the power of their common sense, and they know "something is rotten in Denmark" when it comes to our last election. Or, to put it in the far more elegant words of the author: "Joe Biden was inaugurated not as the forty-sixth president of the American constitutional republic, but as the first president of the American elite oligarchy." He is right.

But the "credentialed elite" and the cultic coven of "experts" told us there was no evidence of election fraud. When the President's attorneys provided the evidence, the experts told us the fraud "wasn't systematic." When widespread examples were presented, the experts pivoted to claim that the fraud "wasn't sufficient" to overturn the election. Yet even that cannot be known, when most courts refused to hear the evidence of fraud, and the highest court in the land abnegated its responsibility to adjudicate this critical dispute that drew in nearly all of the states.

The author shows that such expert-driven browbeating and subterfuge are hardly new. They are the product of a long leftist march through America's institutions, beginning in academia but hardly ending there. He shows that America's elite experts are the enemies of that innate American common sense.

This work is important for several reasons. First, it is timely. We must document the state of affairs now given how perilous the condition of the republic is. Secondly, it is a work in the style that I favor myself—concise and open to the broadest of audiences, with a perpetual focus on the most important question of all: So what? And lastly, *The New Civil War* is a crie de coeur that lays out what the New Left has wrought and what it will demand of us to stop their radical plans without us falling at each other's throats in a civil war once more.

The challenge for us "restorationists," as the author calls us, is to be as committed to victory as are the progressives we face, but without resorting to the scorched-earth tactics they so readily deploy against all who stand in their way. We are witnessing the establishment of a post-republican United States. Our job is to build the "nonelite supermajority" that Donald Trump identified for us in 2016 and which propelled him to the highest office in the land. Otherwise, we will lose America or be condemned to real civil war.

Sebastian Gorka, PhD,
Former Strategist to President Trump
Host of *America First*

1

THE WAR WITHIN

BATTLE LINES DRAWN

The United States is living through a national trauma. Progressives hell-bent on transformation and patriots loyal to the American constitutional tradition are locked in a struggle for the nation's soul. Progressive passion and patriotic fervor both entered the 2020 election strong enough to survive an electoral defeat yet weak enough to ensure that the struggle would continue. Postelection, no progressive believes that their transformation is complete. Most patriots believe that their side has yet to engage fully. The warring sides may not agree on much, but they do agree that the conflict is far from over.

In fact, 2020 was a year in which the conflict spread. Neutral space dwindled. Though few realized it at the time, and many remain mired in denial, the United States jettisoned the rule of law and ceased functioning as a republic in mid-March 2020. From that point forward—I write with no end in sight—many states have been governed as dictatorships. Laws change overnight at the whim of executive decision makers, derived loosely from the utterances of selected elite experts. The only limiting requirement is that each new whim must claim to "follow the science" of public health.

The 2020 election might have offered a referendum on this new expert-driven, elite, oligarchic dictatorship had those same elite oligarchs not seized control of the electoral system. They suppressed news, changed rules, eliminated security measures, conducted secretive tabulations, and reported anomalous results. Some of their moves were legal, some of dubious legality, some clearly illegal. The net result of their machinations was an election-themed bit of performance art. It conveyed the illusion of participation while precluding anything that might have qualified as a remotely free and fair election. Their production was rigged to generate a preordained result—nominally in favor of Joe Biden, but actually in favor of oligarchic progressivism.

Far from a referendum on public opinion, the 2020 election was a demonstration of elite power. For those who might have missed the point, an information-age "seizure of the airwaves" denied communications access to President Trump and his supporters, labeled them subversive, and vowed to make their exclusion permanent. Congressional Democrats announced that they would stage a political show trial of the leader they'd worked so hard to depose—for the sole and explicit purpose of ensuring that the American people could never return him to power. Tens of thousands of troops poured into Washington in the days before Biden's inauguration. The resulting visual looked far more like an elitist coup staged to "save a country from itself" than a constitutional republic cheering its newly elected leader. To millions of patriotic Americans, that's precisely how it felt. For the first time in American history, power was seized rather than transferred. The apparent legality of the seizure does little to alter its essence; it simply highlights the debasement of the elite American institutions charged with assessing legality.

Thanks in large part to the weakened rule of law, 2020's was an election unlike any other. Patriots and progressives agreed that one of our leading political factions was undermining the electoral legitimacy central to the American republic. They disagreed bitterly as to which faction it was. Over forty states, split into two camps, asked the Supreme Court to adjudicate. The nine justices charged as the ultimate arbiters of peaceful conflict resolution told them, in effect, to take their fight elsewhere. It's hard to think of a more dangerous—or more feckless—abdication. When nonviolent resolution mechanisms are unavailable, conflict inevitably becomes violent. When elections and courts lack integrity, mobs and warlords take their place.

America's downward spiral accelerated. As congress counted electoral votes, a mob entered the Capitol building, vandalized federal property, and terrified government workers and officials. At least four people died. Many were injured. Condemnation was quick and unanimous. No one defended the mob.

That apparent unanimity was a dangerous illusion. When it comes to mob violence, (as on so many other issues), patriots and progressives operate in different moral spheres. Patriotic Americans recognize that the commonalities among mobs far outweigh their differences. Whether a mob identifies with the Left or the Right, cites religious or economic motivation, or asserts specific or general grievances, it will inevitably converge on a scapegoat (most often, but hardly always, the Jews). Healthy societies condemn all mob violence. Diseased societies equivocate, tolerate some mobs, abandon the scapegoat, and eventually collapse beneath the weight of a movement that cannot be appeased.

Patriotic Americans understand that mobs, demonstrations giving cover to mobs, and apologists excusing "sympathetic" mobs threaten society. Leading progressives tolerate—and some even deploy—mobs that spout progressive pieties. Though mob violence has been part of American life for over seven years, progressives spread the pernicious lie that the Capitol Building mob represented something new. It didn't. Since 2013, progressive convulsions, conflagrations, and occupations have wracked Ferguson, Baltimore, Charlotte, Atlanta, New York, Washington, Los Angeles, Minneapolis, Seattle, Portland, Kenosha, and other American cities. Progressive mobs have targeted police, vandalized businesses, attacked citizens, and destroyed lives. Progressive mobs have charged the Supreme Court and the White House, and confronted members of Congress in their own office buildings. Progressive mobs have laid siege to federal buildings and courthouses, toppled statues and monuments, burned Bibles, and defaced churches and synagogues.

Progressive political and media leaders have done more than merely downplay these mobs. They've vilified President Trump for issuing blanket condemnations of violence that equate organizations they like with those they despise. Their outrage at the Capitol Building mob arose because its stated grievances challenged the progressive agenda rather than supporting it—and because it threatened and terrified elite members of Congress rather than their hardworking constituents.

Worse, the sudden progressive aversion to mob violence was used to justify unprecedented actions: Congressional Democrats imperiled national security by attempting to interfere with the military chain of command. Then they impeached the president in sham hearings shorn of even the pretense of fact finding, due process, or equal protection. Tech giants made rapid, bold, systematic moves to silence voices opposed to progressivism—steps they'd steadfastly refused to take against recognized terrorist organizations—leaving Iran's Ayatollah Khamenei with greater access to American social media than President Trump.

On inaugural day, many specifics about the Capitol building mob remained unknown. Two weeks of progressive responses, however, bore all the hallmarks of a false-flag operation planned to justify repression, the consolidation of power, and the criminalization of politics. Biden himself entered office speaking of truth while regurgitating progressive lies, and calling for unity while giving no one other than progressives reason to answer his call. His first few hours in office demonstrated that he defined "unity" as universal compliance with the progressive agenda. His inaugural address left no doubt that the "dark winter" he'd promised on the campaign trail had descended upon America.

America's internal conflict has entered its next phase. Progressives are moving quickly to cement their transformation of the country's beliefs, attitudes, values, language, social structures, economic models, and government organization. Patriotic Americans are recognizing that conservatism failed to conserve much of anything—including the Constitution. Documents, even revered documents, have no life of their own. The Constitution lives or dies through the institutions it creates and enables. If those institutions redefine themselves to suit their own tastes, the document can retire. The institutions of contemporary American life bear little resemblance to those capable of breathing life into a constitutional republic.

With each passing year, more and more Americans who'd prefer to remain apolitical find themselves facing an uncomfortable reality:

when an ascendant faction launches a revolution around you, you're either with the revolutionaries or with the regime. In the not-too-distant future, you'll find yourself living in either an America transformed or an America restored. You can't ride it out without showing (at least) tacit support for one of the sides. Might as well think about which side you prefer.

Is our struggle a civil war or a revolution? Were I a progressive seeking to transform America, I would gush about our glorious revolution. As a patriotic American proud of America's founding ideals and glorious history, I choke at the tragedy of our second civil war. Only time will tell whether I've chosen the right label. Perhaps their revolution will succeed. Our victory is hardly inevitable. Faith may assure us that good will prevail over evil in the long run, but history teaches that evil can inflict great pain along the way.

Brutal leaders and cruel ideologies have shaped much of world history. When they're ascendant, republics fall, freedom evaporates, scarcity dominates, violence rages, and people suffer. America has been hurtling in that direction for over a decade; it entered free fall in March 2020. If the progressive transformation succeeds, it will be long before we emerge. Tragic? Absolutely. Unthinkable? Hardly. Just ask a Venezuelan.

Better yet, ask an Eastern European. A mere three decades ago, first the Warsaw Pact, then the Soviet Union, collapsed in the blink of an eye. We saw them as fierce adversaries when George H.W. Bush entered the White House; they were gone by the time Bill Clinton defeated his bid for reelection. Transformation can rewrite the rules of society overnight.

You can't defeat what you can't understand. That's why every good patriot must understand progressivism—where it originated, how it grew, what it preaches, and what it hopes to accomplish.

PROGRESSIVISM

Progressivism is both American and anti-American—a young, twenty-first-century incarnation of Western leftism with a particularly dark view of the US and its 1789 Constitution. Progressives believe that America's true birth occurred in 1619, with the importation of the first African slave. Conceived in this travesty, the new nation eventually emerged to impose its stifling Judeo-Christian morality and the deeply inequitable Anglo-American legal tradition on anyone who had the misfortune of falling beneath its sway. Progressives seek to transform this oppressive, arrogant, conceited, hypocritical behemoth into a force for what they see as a higher, enlightened, evolved good.

Like all leftist movements, progressivism is utopian and elitist. Progressives believe that if we can perfect society, humanity will rise to the occasion. Of course, their shock troops will have to break some heads, spread some misery, and create some injustice along the way to that utopia—but since the ends justify the means, we'd be wrong to complain. A perfected society will bring us all to the next level of enlightenment and justice, living in harmony with each other and with nature.

It's a deeply seductive message. Millions of Americans with no clear understanding of progressivism have come to think of themselves as progressives. Most of them have been duped. I was. I learned the hard way that these goals are worse than unachievable. They're outright lies. Not only can't progressivism deliver them, most hard-core ideological progressives don't value them. Their true goal is to collect dictatorial power while feeling morally superior.

That truth is not hard to see—if you're willing to look. The progressive formula for perfecting society is entirely self-serving: trust the experts! To progressives, enlightened elite opinion provides a guiding light for humanity. That's because—not surprisingly—our elite is overwhelmingly progressive. If there's a conduit for creating a narrative, writing a rule, telling a story, or circulating information, voices committed to progressivism overwhelm those committed to traditional American ideals and values. In the eyes of those progressive storytellers and rule-writers, any expert who rejects the progressive consensus cannot truly qualify as an expert.

Progressives dominate the mechanisms for credentialing and promoting experts. Progressives select only the finest progressive minds to promote into positions of power and prestige. Once there, progressives can appeal to authority. They can then deride Americans who insist that their authorities conform to common sense—or honor the Constitution—for refusing to accept "science" or "the data."

Though many seduced Americans consider themselves progressives, only an elite core understands progressive ideology. No surprise there, because Americans are a compassionate people, and the progressivism of America's contemptuous elite is extraordinarily cruel.

Progressives like to cast their attempts to make poverty a little less uncomfortable as compassionate. Nonsense. Opportunity, and opportunity alone, breeds social and economic mobility—handing the poor a dignified way out of poverty. Opportunity requires a robust, growth-oriented economy, jobs, training, and educational opportunities. Progressives despise the free-market capitalism that promotes economic growth and jobs, view internships and mentoring programs as exploitation, and reject school choice for all but the very wealthy. Progressive economics preaches division and distribution. Progressives decry any attempts to inculcate responsible behavior and positive cultural values. Progressivism seeks to keep the poor mired in poverty, addicted to government handouts, terrified of advancement—and at arm's length.

Progressives are equally cruel to America's minority communities. Each of these communities has distinct strengths and faces unique challenges. Each boasts a diverse array of voices, opinions, and priorities. Progressives approach them each as monoliths—designating their angriest, least constructive elements as authentic, while denigrating those most eager to seek the American dream.

Our black community is suffering from the collapse of its family structure and a weakening of its historic faith. Young black men are disproportionately likely both to commit and to be victims of violent crime—and consequently to be mistaken for perpetrators or intended victims. Black neighborhoods remain among America most dangerous, driving out investment, making jobs scarce, and yielding poor public schools. A compassionate approach would seek ways to strengthen families and churches, improve neighborhood safety, promote investment, and enhance school choice, training programs, and internship opportunities. Progressives work overtime against these goals. They seek to reduce policing and eliminate the nuclear family, deter investment, and maintain rigid control over school placement.

Our Latino community is following in the footsteps of so many wonderful immigrant communities of the American past. Its greatest needs are stability and Americanization. New arrivals must learn English, civics, American history, and entrepreneurship. Progressives oppose all of those objectives. Instead, they seek to flood Latino neighborhoods with a constant stream of poorly vetted new arrivals, importing to America the gang violence so many decent Latinos fled.

America's Muslims came here to escape the violence and oppression rampant in Muslim-majority countries. Compassion would help them learn to synthesize their culture with the American mainstream, integrating notions of individual liberty and personal responsibility first developed in the Christian West. Progressives embrace only the most outraged, victimized Muslim voices—leaders and organizations that radicalize first-generation Muslims, cruelly turning them into caricatures of the very people their parents fled.

Our diverse Asian immigrants arrive believing deeply in the American dream. Their communities engage in quiet Americanization, fostering family, education, and hard work. A compassionate approach would recognize them as an asset to America, provide them with the assistance they need, and laud their cultural success. Progressives hold the Asian commitment to the American dream in contempt; they seek ways to degrade schools that reward excellence, downplay earned merit, and submit Asians to debilitating quotas.

Progressive cruelty permeates American society. Its promotion of gender reassignment surgery and hormone therapy for sexually uncertain adolescents is child abuse. Its gleeful insistence that nuns fund abortion and that all must celebrate same-sex marriage is anti-Christian bigotry. Its fixation on Jewish power and its campaign of double standards, demonization, and delegitimization of the Jewish State are antisemitic. Its injection of men-who-identify-as-female into women's shelters, sports, and bathrooms is misogyny. In the midst of a pandemic, progressives are unable to see a photo of people enjoying life, family, and community without shouting, "There ought to be a law against that!"

Ideological progressivism has long been a cult of elitism and expertise; it's now verging on becoming a full-blown religion. Its adherents preach a well-defined and distinctive moral code. They seek to excommunicate blasphemers, questioners, doubters, and deniers. They're extremely intolerant of those who follow old-time religions. Their views of biology, sex, race, gender, the supernatural, the start of life, and the place of humanity within nature set them apart from other faiths. They have a particularly well-

-developed eschatology—an end of times borne of humanity's sins against the global climate.

Political progressivism has swallowed politicians who'd built long careers posing as pragmatic moderates—from Joe Biden on down. Even while asking America, "Do I look like a radical socialist?" Biden promised to complete the progressive transformation Barack Obama had left unfinished. The message was clear to anyone willing to hear it: his goal was deeply radical, even if not classically socialist.

The progressive outrages hit new highs with a 2020 election structured to invite fraud at every juncture. Because the law presumes that government actions are proper unless proved otherwise, no one ever had to justify the system. Legal presumptions, however, cannot hide the truth. A system combining high stakes, inflamed passions, numerous opportunities to cheat, low probabilities of detection, and meager penalties is a system designed without credibility. No surprise that the results it produced were literally incredible; the data defy statistical expectations, historical experience, and political logic.

A country prepared to pretend that the 2020 election was free and fair will never again experience a free and fair election. The consent of the governed has given way to enlightened elite opinion. Joe Biden was inaugurated not as the forty-sixth president of the American constitutional republic, but as the first president of an American elitist oligarchy.

Biden is a classically perfect choice to lead such a government: a doddering grandfatherly figure with no independent support base behind whom progressive factions, warlords, and oligarchs can jostle for power. The demographic entitlement used to foist Kamala Harris onto his ticket was only the opening salvo. Harris's total reliance on the progressive donors, activists, and organizations who pushed her forward—and her demonstrable inability to assemble any popular support of her own—keeps the real power behind the scenes. Though many in the progressive base resent Biden and Harris as inauthentic, the elites appreciate the deniability these weak careerist hacks provide to the blissfully seduced Americans whose awakening would render the progressive transformation impossible. The primary assignment of the Biden/Harris administration is to keep them sedated while the country they love morphs into something unrecognizable.

RESTORATIONISM

In 2020, the United States "evolved" beyond the rule of law and veered sharply onto the path of fallen republics. It never could have done so had its institutions remained grounded in its constitutional ideals. They hadn't. Progressives had spent decades marching through America's institutions while conservatives stood on the sidelines objecting politely. With a weak defense and no offense, conservatives ceded every inch of institutional territory. Progressives now control academia, K-12 education, media, the civil service, much of the judiciary, more than a handful of states, most professional organizations, Hollywood, Silicon Valley, much of Wall Street, and several of our most important industries. From top to bottom, public and private, America's great institutions have become a source of deep embarrassment. Not a single one can point with pride to its performance in the twenty-first century. Conservatism is finished. You can't conserve what you've already lost.

Our institutions need not remain lost forever. The challenge before us is to restore them. Patriots who support the constitutional regime have become countercultural counterrevolutionaries—American restorationists. Restorationism may agree with conservatism on many policy issues, but it's hardly conservative in temperament. Restorationists must learn to recognize the weapons progressives deploy—and master those tailored to suitable defense and counterattack. Restoration requires both a solid defense and a penetrating offense.

The need for an American restorationist movement has never been greater than it is today. When our constitutionally guaranteed republican form of government fades into governance at the manipulation of the elite, the rest of the Constitution fades into a set of dated, historically interesting guidelines. Today's Americans enjoy stunningly few true freedoms or rights. Religious exercise, speech, press, assembly, bearing arms, privacy and security, equal protection, and due process have all become conditioned upon the dictates of progressive morality and government policy. A porous Constitution provides little protection from the progressive onslaught. The challenge facing patriotic Americans today is—quite literally—the restoration of the American republic.

Restoration is hard work, particularly given the current configuration of power. But beneath the elite overlords, tens of millions of patriots remain committed to the ideals of America's founding. Many more will join us as they come to understand what progressivism truly represents. The republican spirit persists even in a fallen republic. The roots of the republic remain planted around the country. Restoration is achievable. A second American republic can arise.

We can't hope to restore America unless we understand how we lost it. Much as it's taken us decades of inattention to squander the great republic our founders bequeathed us, it will take us decades of concerted effort to get it back. It won't be easy.

Our constitutional regime was firmly in charge as recently as twenty years ago. The 1990s featured bitter partisan disputes about matters of public policy, but no sizable American faction ventured into the overt anti-Americanism that colors contemporary progressivism. Much has changed since then. The twenty-first century has been brutal. The United States has become a nation fully at war with itself.

Granted, not enough of us are getting shot for it to be a traditional war. Yet. But we have always been an exceptional nation. Our disintegration into warring camps has been similarly exceptional. Relatively few of our fellow Americans want us dead.

A sizable number of America's progressives, however, want us destroyed, humbled, reeducated, repentant, and submissive. They're perfectly happy defaming us, destroying our reputations, getting us fired and evicted, making us toxic as social connections, depleting our resources, terrifying us, shuttering our businesses, breaking up our families, terrifying our kids, and driving us into the streets. Then, when we concede the error of our ways, they'll force someone else to pay for our health care, forgive a couple of the loans their actions or policies made it impossible for us to repay, put us on the dole, and expect us to gush with gratitude about their largesse.

The rapid growth and stunning pervasiveness of progressivism has led us into a civil war. America's first civil war arose because a compromise between two fundamentally incompatible ethical, economic, and social systems became untenable. We're heading toward a similar collapse today, with two fundamentally incompatible ethical, economic, and social systems coexisting uneasily. It's not just that we disagree about policy. Progressives and restorationists have incompatible values and divergent views of reality. We interpret events differently. We define words differently. Though it all sounds like English, progressives and restorationists don't speak the same language.

The progressive views of the world, of justice, of rights, of economics, and of society are incompatible with those of traditional America. In the long run, one will give way to the other. Will America remain the bold, exceptional experiment in individualism, personal responsibility, compassion, opportunity, Judeo-Christian morality, and the Anglo-American tradition it was founded to be? Or will progressivism transform it into something fundamentally different and profoundly cruel? To restore America, we must defeat progressivism as surely as we defeated its cruel predecessors, fascism and communism.

Restorationism is a movement for traditional, patriotic Americans who want to win decisively. Americans who want to restore traditional American values. Americans who understand that liberty is only possible among those who can trust their neighbors to behave responsibly and ethically. Americans who understand that the founding of the United States marked the single greatest victory for individual freedom in all of human history. Americans who know that America has given far more to the world than it has ever asked in return.

We American restorationists need to develop, master, and deploy strategies capable of winning. We need strategies that can both restore the country at large and handle our relationships with the progressives in our own lives. We need to do it without burning down the country we love and without losing the people we love. In short, we need a nonviolent strategy capable of persuading our fellow Americans that they've been badly misled.

First, remember who we are: *we are Americans*! Second, know the enemy: progressivism seeks to undermine our morality and our sanity. Third, recognize the weapons deployed against us: deconstruction, fabrication, and projection—or lies, lies, lies. Fourth, master the arsenal of defense and counterattack: definition, examination, and reflection—call them out on their lies.

We'll dive into details later. Knowledge of the enemy must precede weapons training. We can't know the enemy without studying its home. The restoration of America must begin with an understanding of campus life and culture. That's where progressivism was conceived, born, and raised to maturity. That's where progressivism seduced and perverted so many of America's most idealistic youth. That's where it began its long march through America's institutions.

I've studied progressivism from the inside. Two decades living deep inside academia taught me to recognize the chasm dividing academic mythology from the true incentives guiding campus life. A clear view of academia provides the key to understanding—and to defeating—progressivism.

Nothing I experienced on campus was particularly egregious. That's good. If my adventures in academia had been unusual, they couldn't serve the purpose I need them to serve. Any institution can produce outliers. What makes my personal experiences worth relating is precisely that they were mundane and representative—and even better, that most of them arose in the least controversial corner of American higher education. I've had to reconstruct some specifics and conversations and change some names, but the academic adventures I'm about to share are all very real.

2

THE CULT OF EXPERTISE

THE CREDENTIALED ELITE

Here's my story. Or part of it, anyway. I started young—very young. By my midtwenties, I'd become a full-fledged member of America's biggest, best, and most socially acceptable cult: the cult of expertise. The Credentialed Elite. I loved it. Until I asked too many questions, broke too many rules, and found myself exiled. If you want to understand what's happened to America over the past few decades, you need to understand my cult.

The Credentialed Elite are the most entitled members of contemporary American society—and contemporary American society embodies a very entitled culture. Members of the Credentialed Elite are entitled to high salaries, exceptional benefits, unrivaled job security, minimal concrete responsibilities, and near-total freedom in their work. They're entitled to secure funding without promising or delivering results. They're entitled to be accepted as superiors, whose motives are unassailable and whose work is beyond reproach. They're entitled to be free of opinions they disdain.

The Credentialed Elite created an entire self-serving myth system, hypnotized itself into believing that it was gospel truth, then foisted it upon America. In this elite mythology, selfless trained experts serve the causes of truth, justice, and fairness. Acting out of pure benevolence, these experts carve out a few hours a week to work with our young—whom we send eagerly to indoctrination centers called universities. Under the guise of teaching them how to think, experts instill in them both a sense of superiority and a fear of feeling stupid. Nothing is stupider than questioning accepted wisdom.

Once on campus, America's children learn that credentials are more important than experience, that theory trumps practice, that enlightened elite opinion is always correct, and that the unenlightened masses are immoral fools. They learn that it's fine to stand out in a crowd—if it's a crowd of your inferiors. They learn to fear nothing more than appearing inferior to those around them. Credentialed Elite experts do us the favor of beating the innate curiosity out of our young, teaching them to be risk averse in speech and in thought.

By the time our kids finish their undergraduate work, we expect them to understand that there's nothing more impressive than an advanced degree, and that those who possess advanced degrees alone may set the terms of discourse. The Credentialed Elite determines what we can discuss, what we can think, and which young people it invites to join the club.

The Credentialed Elite needs these indoctrination centers because, like any other movement or group, it must perpetuate itself. While it favors its own children, it's more than happy to absorb the children of others. Universities provide its breeding ground. Because universities alone can grant credentials, universities alone determine who can join the Credentialed Elite. Undergrad programs provide the great sort. Those who make the cut get invited into the inner sanctum: graduate and professional schools. That's where they train to perpetuate the cult. Where they master the specialized jargon that lets cult members identify each other and shun outsiders. Where they learn the how to dominate American society. Where they learn how to operate as members of the Credentialed Elite. Upon learning the basics, they reenter American society as the Newly Credentialed.

Each of these Newly Credentialed must choose a specialization. Some become "complexifiers." They assume the critical task of making simple things appear complicated. The more confusing, the better. Nothing makes the Credentialed Elite happier than lengthy, incomprehensible expressions of concepts that every preschooler understands—except, of course, for lengthy, incomprehensible explanations of why obvious truths that every preschooler understands are, in fact, incorrect.

The key task of these complexifiers is to ensure that no one outside the Credentialed Elite can possibly understand what they're saying or why they took the time to say it. Complexity and incomprehensibility are central to the self-image of the Credentialed Elite. Without them, the entire cult would crumble into insignificance. And nothing—nothing!—scares the Credentialed Elite more than insignificance.

Others among the Newly Credentialed become "translators." Their task is to translate the complexifiers' work into language that those lacking credentials can almost—but never quite—comprehend.

Another set of the Newly Credentialed become "debaters." They assume the task of fighting about the translations—and the different implications of competing translations. Debaters enhance the value of translators. Debaters create a lucrative market for complexifiers and translators—as well as for themselves.

Finally, a select few of the Newly Credentialed become "marketers." They assume the most important task of all. They ensure that the masses understand how important the Credentialed Elite are. How lucky American society is to have them. Why the services of the Credentialed Elite are a bargain at any price. Why it's so important for America to trust the experts.

These marketers are particularly important in reaching the Terrified Minorities, the Americans who feel that the community to which they belong has not yet fully achieved the American dream. Without the help of marketers, the Terrified Minorities would lose their fear and appreciate America's bounty. They might recognize that the dream is within reach and just as available to their communities as it has been to others. Marketers are responsible for keeping them terrified of the America they wish to join, mired in a sense of victimhood, and turning to the Credentialed Elite for help.

The Credentialed Elite has learned to weaponize Terrified Minorities to deploy against their true enemy: the American Ambitious—those lacking advanced degrees who still run businesses, work hard, perhaps get wealthy. The American Ambitious are distasteful at best, likely dangerous. Many of them seem to like shooting things. Keeping a safe distance is critical. Yet many among the American Ambitious refuse to acknowledge their place in the pecking order. They deny their own inferiority. The Terrified Minorities are also distasteful, of course, but they're far easier to keep at arm's length. They know their place. They would never think of themselves as equal to the Credentialed Elite.

Such concerns are beyond the purview of the Newly Credentialed. In fact, if enough of the Newly Credentialed understood what they were doing, some might recoil in horror before investing their own prestige in the corrupt system. No, far better to keep the Newly Credentialed in the dark, where many will stay throughout their entire careers.

In the meantime, life is grand in the cult of expertise—great for the Credentialed Elite. The money is good. The prestige is better. The sense of self-importance is unrivaled. Complexify. Translate. Debate. Market. Terrify the minorities. Patronize the ambitious. What could be better?

As with all cults, however, it has a downside, a dark secret, a price for admission. All candidates for Credentialed Elite status must check their common sense at the door. Anyone found exercising common sense in or around a university risks ostracism or expulsion.

Me? I made the cut. I spent most of two decades on elite campuses, first at Columbia, then at UCLA, then at USC, then at Georgetown, with an occasional cameo at Carnegie Mellon. I became a full-fledged member of the Credentialed Elite. But along the way, something went wrong. I tried to check my common sense at the door. I tried hard. I checked what I could, but some of it clung to me—as if it were a gun or God or something. That made me dangerous. I learned the rules and dared to question them.

I stared long and hard at things that didn't seem to make sense. I questioned methodology when all that was supposed to matter was outcome. I became the sort of cult member who might go rogue. I was sent to a corner, relegated to the periphery, tossed to the curb—where, indeed, I went rogue. Turns out, those who judged me had not been wrong. They knew a threat when they saw one—long before I understood how or why I threatened them.

I stand today as an unrepentant member of the Renegade Credentialed: a full-fledged, well-trained, elite expert prepared to reveal the deep, dark secrets that allow the cult to function. Like many renegades, I entered my cult eagerly and enthusiastically, able to see its many strengths and pleased to believe the myths of its benevolent grandeur. Over the decades, I've learned that though many of the strengths provide genuine benefits, most of the myths are pernicious lies spread to cover the antisocial devastation academia has wrought upon the very fabric of American life.

FREEING NELSON MANDELA

I didn't join the cult planning to restore America. I arrived on campus as a whiz kid and a wannabe radical. The whiz kid stuff came easy. I hated high school enough to know that the easiest way out was to plow through the material quickly and just be done with it. So I did. I hit campus at sixteen and immediately set off to find some radicals—or even better, hippies. I did that, too. I learned rather quickly that fitting in was far harder than finding them. That, I couldn't do—not for lack of trying, and not for lack of commitment to the cause. I never fit in with the radicals because I had an annoying habit of trying to get things to make sense.

Walking across campus during my very first month, I met a bunch of folks badmouthing Soviet communism and American capitalism. Twin evils, they said. They had better ideas: Ideas about freeing humanity from its bonds of slavery. Ideas that would transcend national boundaries. Ideas that would end greed and make sure that everyone had the food, shelter, and care they needed. It sounded good. I subscribed to their magazine. *Worker's Vanguard* introduced me to committed Trotskyism. By the end of the first issue, I was deeply troubled.

It was my first real lesson in hard-left radicalism. Plenty of dangerous people excel at spotting genuine injustice and deep systemic problems. That's the bait they use to hook well-intentioned kids—like me. Once caught, too few kids ask whether those "concerned" radicals really want to make things better; it's enough to know that they've identified legitimate problems to which they claim to have solutions. It's a classically tragic confusion of ends and means. Most leftist proposals involve changing human nature, upending the economy, restructuring society, and reordering the world—none of which are remotely possible. The predictable result of trying is an angry, brutal totalitarianism. Radicals who rise to power invariably make life far, far worse for almost everyone than it was under the "unjust" regime they displaced. They do, however, get to claim moral superiority while seizing power and imposing misery.

I might have been among those unquestioning kids had I begun my journey with a group somewhat subtler than Young Spartacus. After that encounter, I became a bit more circumspect. But only a bit. Toward the end of my freshman year, I found a group that sounded far less dangerous: Students against Militarism (SAM). Antimilitarism was the opposite of dangerous, right?

My first SAM event was a protest against President Reagan's support for the right-wing government of El Salvador. Reagan wanted to start a third world war that would inevitably lead to a nuclear conflagration and the annihilation of all life on the planet. My new friends and I thought that sounded like a bad idea. We opposed militarism. What better way to show it than by standing in the middle of campus, drinking beer, waving signs, and chanting? It was exciting, exhilarating. I was part of the movement! We'd bring down Reagan the way we'd brought down LBJ and Nixon! Being part of the movement rocked. I could take credit for bringing down two presidents who fell before my bar mitzvah.

I got to know the other SAM members. I said that we shouldn't be involved in Central America. No more Vietnams! Some of them agreed with me. Most of them added that we were on the wrong side. That confused me. How would switching sides reduce militarism? Answer: if you have to ask, you're part of the problem. It took me decades to figure it out, but it appears that I am indeed part of the problem.

Four years later, I helped my SAM friends occupy a building. Technically, we were only part of the occupation, operating beneath the umbrella of the Coalition for a Free South Africa. We'd devised a plan to end apartheid. We were going to sleep on the steps of Hamilton Hall until Columbia divested $6 million in Coca-Cola stock and a handful of other equity holdings. If that didn't end apartheid, nothing would.

It was a good plan—and an even better time. The music was great. Local restaurants brought us free food. Campus security made it safe to sleep outside. Campus custodians made sure we had clean bathrooms. Also, our righteous indignation burned with the intensity of a million suns. We were championing the cause of justice! We got great press coverage—lots of it. We were on the news. Every channel. Every night. So we waved signs: "No Justice, No Peace!" "End Apartheid Now!" "Free Nelson Mandela!" "Hi, Mom!" Years before anyone coined the term "social justice warrior," we were warriors for justice.

I had some problems with our guest speakers, though. It seems that we opened the podium to everyone with a grievance. In 1980s New York City, that was a pretty long list. Jesse Jackson trekked all the way to Hymietown just to grace us with his presence. We welcomed advocates for the Sandinista, the IRA, the PLO, and many other fine organizations from around the world. The Columbia Tenant's

Organization explained why having the university as your landlord was exactly like living under apartheid. I was skeptical. Still, it was considered rude to ask questions.

After about two weeks, the crowds began to thin. With finals looming, some of the protestors thought that it might be a good idea to crack a book. I approached the protest's leaders, most of whom were old friends from SAM. They'd set their headquarters in the beautiful, recently renovated room that our irredeemably racist university had named the Malcolm X Lounge. At the risk of being rude, I decided to ask some questions:

"Uh, guys? I wanted to ask you about some of the speakers. We're supposed to be a coalition here. If PLO and NORAID want to help end apartheid, I guess it's okay to have them on board. But they're terrorist organizations. Doesn't it cut against the nature of a coalition to impose their views on the rest of us?"

They stared at each other, then at me. The answer, apparently, was easy. "Lots of our people support them. They're fighting injustice."

"Okay, fine," I said. "But look at what they're saying. Every speaker insists that the folks they're fighting are as evil as the apartheid regime. That's the opposite of our message! Our whole point is that apartheid is a unique evil! They're saying that it's not remotely unique. They're turning apartheid into a synonym for mean."

That drew puzzled looks. "Yeah. Lots of our people support them. They're fighting injustice."

I was sensing a party line not to be questioned. "All right," I said. "One more thing. We're hemorrhaging supporters. We all know that the university can't make a divestment decision until the trustees meet this summer. It's time to declare victory while we've still got the press. Go out strong. Say that we're confident that the trustees have heard our message and will do the right thing. Then let everyone go study for finals."

Again, the response was easy and unanimous. "We can't declare victory. We haven't won. We won't win until the university divests."

"Are you kidding?" I asked. I was in the zone. "Divestment is symbolic. We don't win if the university sells some stocks. We win when the apartheid regime crumbles, and Nelson Mandela becomes president of a free South Africa."

Silence. The scary kind of silence. The kind where you know you've just shattered a taboo. Once again, the looks went around the room.

"You know, man, we're sick and tired of you Jews telling us how to run our movement. Either shut up or bail on the cause. You Jews only fight for justice if you can be in charge and cash in."

I suddenly felt very, very uncomfortable. It was a wakeup call. Their casual antisemitism, strategic blindness, and indifference to the sensibilities of their allies hit me hard. Real radicals are radical for the sake of radicalism, not for the sake of justice. What they value is power. Turns out, "question authority" is an ambiguous slogan. To me, it was supposed to mean that those handed authority must continually prove themselves worthy of our trust. To real leftist radicals it means challenging today's authority, installing authorities they prefer, then forcing everyone else to shut up and comply. That's precisely why four years of anti-Trump insurrectionist resistance gave way to a call for "unity" the moment the progressives seized control.

Back then though, all I realized was that I'd been seduced. I wanted to believe I was fighting injustice, when all I was really doing was empowering radical leftists. Shut up or bail? The choice was easy. I've never been very good at shutting up. I bailed. Not on the cause of fighting injustice, mind you. On SAM.

Ten days later, a couple of dozen diehards marched uptown to proclaim victory. No headliners. No press coverage. Columbia divested that summer. Nelson Mandela spent another four years in jail. Reagan's policy of constructive engagement, not campus divestment campaigns, ended apartheid. Who would have guessed? Other than Reagan, I suppose. Maybe the people who voted for him. Not us.

At UCLA, I was one of the Students for a Nuclear Free Society. We had faculty members researching elements of Reagan's Strategic Defense Initiative (SDI)—Star Wars! Worse, the university was offering a course explicitly covering SDI—a course designed to make it appear achievable! The topics that it promised to cover were all geared toward getting the system to work. What about the many prominent software engineers who had proved that quality assurance issues doomed the system to failure? What about their work showing that a necessarily imperfect missile defense system would make us arrogant, prone to miscalculation, and much more likely to destroy the world? Their voices were being stifled!

We flew into action. The challenge was clear. The situation called for a strongly worded column in the *Daily Bruin*. As a grad student in computer science, I was the obvious choice to write it. So I did. I wrote about the need to include those excluded voices. It ran under the headline "Present Balanced Class." Worst. Radical. Ever.

I joined the USC faculty without having internalized these important lessons of radicalism. I glided easily from my role as a clueless radical grad student to a new one as a clueless radical professor.

I saw a flier for Students for a Non-Sexist Society, a new organization in need of a faculty sponsor. I volunteered. For the rest of the semester, I attended the meetings, helped run events, even fronted some cash. Then summer came, and the group evaporated. Or so I thought. Nope. They'd found a female faculty advisor and decided they didn't need me anymore. Seems that if you're going to accept male leadership, you might as well be part of a sexist society.

Good radicals have no sense of irony. Or self-awareness.

If I'd been savvier, I'd have noticed a theme. Real radicals know the score. The labels are smokescreens. The honest messages all sound bad:

Let's support the Communists!

Let's neuter the men!

Let's impose our own solutions!

Let's back terrorists!

With messages like those, you'll get the true believers—but only the true believers. You'll never seduce the well-intentioned kids who want to make the world a better place—the kids like me. No, for real radicals, marketing reigns supreme. And none of that truth-in-advertising nonsense. Just the opposite: seduction.

Let's support the Communists becomes let's oppose militarism.

Let's neuter the men becomes let's fight sexism.

Let's impose our own solutions becomes let's fight for social justice.

Let's back terrorist movements becomes let's oppose apartheid.

It really is quite brilliant—and effective. The amusing experiences I had with campus radicals in the 1980s now threaten to destroy the entire country. Their charming hypocrisy, obliviousness, anti-Americanism, sexism, antisemitism, socialism, and authoritarianism has somehow become dark. They were laying the groundwork for twenty-first-century progressivism.

APPROACHING WORLD ORDER

For the record, I also learned some useful things in my classes. Some of them, at least. One class, and one professor, stands out. Saul Mendlovitz, now in his nineties, is not a household name. Though a successful academic by any measure—he's the Dag Hammarskjold

Professor of Peace and World Order Studies at the Rutgers University School of Law—he hasn't even rated his own Wikipedia page (at least as of this writing).

Back when I was an undergrad at Columbia, Saul taught a poli-sci course called "Approaches to World Order," nicknamed "pre--Messiah." Saul was known for his bold vision looking beyond our militaristic, capitalist society toward a just future for the entire planet. Who better to provide practical pointers on fixing the world?

The basic idea behind world order reasoning—of which Saul is a guru—is pretty simple: If you're interested in justice, you need to address problems on a global scale. Solutions necessarily involve reordering the world. Drop the self-interested focus of nationalism, see yourself as a citizen of the planet, convince everyone else to do the same, put in place an appropriate global restructuring plan, and all manner of wonderful things will follow. Easy steps to a utopian existence. Useful skills for a budding Messiah.

We started the semester identifying problems on a global scale: war, poverty, famine, discrimination, environmental degradation. That was fun. Real feel-good stuff. I loved every minute of it. Everyone thought I was Saul's favorite. Star pre-Messiah student? Talk about a bright future!

From diagnosis, we moved on to solutions. Different authors told us how to fix the world. That was even more fun. Sci-fi or poli-sci? It didn't much matter. Messianism was within easy reach.

Then we hit the real messianic part. Saul prescribed the right answers. It was a trap. I fell right in. I asked questions.

Now, let me be clear. I didn't challenge Saul's answers. I didn't suggest that he might be wrong. I simply asked about his methods—how he concluded that the right answers were right.

Mistake. Big mistake.

Saul assigned us an article summarizing studies about the environment. I read it eagerly, studied the charts, and arrived in class fully prepared. The ability to fix the environment seemed like a core messianic skill. I took my training seriously.

Saul opened: "Which study got it right?" I raised my hand. He called on me. "Do we really have enough information? We read a seventeen-page article covering twenty statistical analyses. Wouldn't we have to see the underlying data to know which one is right?" He furrowed his brow, glared at me, and rephrased. "All right, if you're going to get technical. Which one strikes you as being right?"

Even that wasn't quite what he meant. What he meant was "Which one do you think strikes me as being right?"

That question had a clear, well-defined answer: Club of Rome.

The Club of Rome has its own Wikipedia page—as it should. It's an exclusive club restricted to extremely impressive members of the Credentialed Elite. The Club of Rome is a collection of very prestigious experts who've been screaming that the world is on the verge of running out of resources since the early 1970s. When I took Saul's class, they'd only been wrong for about a decade. I was perfectly prepared to believe that they were right, provided they could put forward a persuasive case—which Saul certainly didn't do on their behalf.

It's not surprising that he didn't. The Club of Rome belongs to a long tradition of hysterics worried about resource depletion, dating back a couple of hundred years to Thomas Malthus. This line of experts has an unbroken track record of bringing prestige and seriousness to the wrong side of a debate. Notwithstanding their expertise, the world is not about to run out of resources. Nature is not about to smite us for our profligate ways. Technology and free markets have brought us standards of health, prosperity, and even peace unimaginable in earlier eras. Yes, pollution is a problem, but it's a problem of abundance. From the dawn of history, our biggest problem had been a shortage of food. All of a sudden, we're complaining that there's too much garbage. We've replaced the problems of scarcity with the problems of abundance. And problems of abundance—though surely problematic—are far lesser problems than problems of scarcity. Ah, capitalism!

Try telling that to the Club of Rome. Or to Saul. Or to any of the folks pushing today's climate change theology. I didn't have to. That would have meant challenging Saul's conclusion as well as his methods. I was already in enough trouble. Club of Rome was the answer Saul wanted, and plenty of students were willing to give it to him. I wasn't among them. It dawned on me that becoming the Messiah might be harder than it looked.

It didn't get any better after that. Saul waxed indignant about life expectancy in Africa. He showed us a chart. Life expectancy for a male in North America was seventy-two. In Africa it was fifty-four. It reeked of injustice. "Why should there be a difference?" he cried. "Why can't we get these numbers to be the same? What can we do to bring one number up or the other down?" I raised my hand. He called on me. "We could kill a lot of North American baby boys," I suggested. Would have brought that seventy-two way down—fast.

That was the last time he called on me. After that, no one thought I was his favorite. If my grade was any indication, they got that right. Saul taught me an important lesson, though: the pre-Messiah label was no joke. Radical leftists like Saul actually believe that a seminar room full of Credentialed Elite experts can fix a world that's been suffering since the fall from Eden. No wonder their ideas invariably lead to angry, brutal totalitarianism. The damn people refuse to fall in line and comply with theoretical constructs!

Saul also taught me a more practical lesson: stick to math and science. If there's no math to back up the content, anything that runs against the official authorized opinion will be deemed wrong—and likely offensive. In college, it cost me some grades. Today, it can lead to life-altering cancellation.

CHECKMATE

A few years later, some friends invited me to an exciting seminar. Their department, which focused on math and computing education, was on the verge of the sort of thing that counts as a major coup among the Credentialed Elite: wooing the impressive Professor Browne away from a far more prestigious department at Yale.

As a twenty-year-old grad student, I was by far the youngest member of the audience. Professor Browne mesmerized the crowd with his statistical analyses of the ways that people learned to use word processors—then considered an advanced piece of software. He detailed the way that he'd set up his study; discussed how he'd carefully divided his subjects into novice, intermediate, and expert groups; and explained his statistical conclusions. It was a masterful performance. I was duly impressed—until I realized that he had omitted one seemingly minor detail.

I raised my hand. My hosts considered the move gauche, but Professor Browne—sport that he was—called on me nonetheless. "You forgot to specify how many subjects you had in each group," I suggested helpfully. "That would be useful in understanding your correlations."

I'd done it again. It wasn't meant to be a trick question. But it was. Professor Browne had tested a total of eleven subjects divided into three groups. His entire expert group consisted of the wife of one of his colleagues.

If you know anything about statistics, you understand that I'd inadvertently and impolitely called him out as a fraud. If you know anything about academia, you understand that I'd embarrassed myself and scandalized my hosts. What kind of pissant grad student thinks he can show up a professor from Yale?

They hired him. It was indeed a coup. All involved concluded that despite being a bright enough young man, I lacked the maturity to appreciate the sort of work that made their department proud. Perhaps, my hosts suggested, I might do better to stick to my own department and my own research.

I tried to comply. I stuck to the Computer Science Department, where I was working on statistical approaches to artificial intelligence. Along the way, I was assigned the task of surveying a topic related to my thesis. I chose to focus on the very first AI challenge anyone had ever posed to a computer: chess.

From day one (technically, 1951) the basic problem plaguing chess-playing computers had been clear: what the computer would really like to do is study all possible chess games to figure out which moves lead to wins and which to losses. That would eliminate all guesswork, and the computer would always make the best move. But there are too many possible chess games for a computer to catalog them all. At some point, the computer has to operate with partial and imperfect information to assess which move is best—just like a human player.

Another thing that's been clear since day one is that there are really only two strategies for collecting that partial information: you can try to teach the computer something about chess and have it consider potential moves and responses "selectively," or you can have it consider all possible moves and all possible responses with "brute force." The tradeoff? Selective approaches can search many moves ahead because they ignore many possible moves—potentially including great moves. Brute force approaches never miss anything, but they can't see very far ahead because they're too busy chasing down nonsense.

That's background. If you know how academics operate, you can immediately guess where we're heading.

By the time I got around to surveying the field in the mid-1980s, the world of computer chess had sorted itself into two highly partisan warring camps. And if you think that the stakes of the midcentury computer chess wars were somewhat lesser than the stakes in the midcentury faceoff between the United States and the Soviet Union, that just means you're not a computer chess warrior—or an academic.

I wasn't a computer chess warrior. I wandered onto that battlefield thinking that chess was useful in studying decision-making, strategy formation, and computing in the presence of incomplete information—in other words, AI. Like most people who wander naively onto battlefields, I was more or less asking to get hurt.

In those days, the great luminary of computer chess was the very credentialed, very elite Professor Hans Berliner of Carnegie Mellon University. One of the world's top correspondence chess players, Berliner had entered the fray in the 1960s extolling the virtues of selective strategies and deriding the simple fools who advocated brute force. It was clear to him that if you wanted a computer to play chess, you had to teach it a lot about chess; no one and nothing could ever achieve competence (much less mastery) brutishly blundering through all possible moves and responses. Berliner wrote many articles making his point emphatically and attempting to shut down research, publication, and funding to those foolish enough to prefer brute force.

Over the years, Berliner had developed several chess programs embodying his ideas and entered virtually every available computer chess tournament. That's where the problem started. The fools pursuing worthless, nonsensical, unpublishable, brute force approaches that should never have been funded beat his entries. Consistently.

Still, Berliner was both a grandmaster and a tenured member of the Credentialed Elite, so he couldn't possibly have been wrong. There was no chance—none—that his less prestigious adversaries were producing superior work, that his publication advice had been exactly backward, or that his funding recommendations had been impeding scientific inquiry. No, at the very worst, his unbroken string of defeats demonstrated that he was moving incrementally in the right direction, while those who got there ahead of him had missed all the critical knowledge to be learned along the way. These are pretty basic rules governing the cult of expertise. Every member of the Credentialed Elite knows them well.

Defeat, however, has a way of focusing the mind—even among the Credentialed Elite. After one-too-many brute force programs defeated his selective searchers, Berliner experienced an epiphany; in the mid-1970s, he began extolling the virtues of brute force approaches and deriding the simple fools who advocated selective searches. What he never did, however, was admit that he'd been wrong. Perhaps he wanted to, but he couldn't. That would have violated the code by which the Credentialed Elite live. I read every one of Berliner's published articles looking for his mea culpa. Never found it. He was good. A true grandmaster of the cult of expertise.

As luck would have it, the postepiphany Berliner got right what the preepiphany Berliner had missed. By the mid-1980s he'd assembled a team of students who capitalized on growing computer power and speed to build a special-purpose chess computer called Hitech, which IBM bought, improved, and renamed Deep Blue. In 1997, Deep Blue won a match against world champion Gary Kasparov.

Vindication! Proof that Berliner's path had been the right one all along—whatever that path may have been.

Meanwhile, I continued meandering naively around the battlefield. I was never much of a chess player, and I'd never thought of chess as anything other than an occasional diversion. My interest in computer chess arose strictly because I saw chess as a model of strategic decision-making, and I was very interested in strategic decision-making. So—fool that I was—that's where I directed my research.

People who actually care about chess tend to spend a lot of time studying openings and endgames. Those are the parts of the chess game that are best understood, and where most aficionados think that chess knowledge and mastery lie. Because they're so well understood, they're also the easiest to teach (even to a computer) and to hard-wire. I chose to look at the midgame. How can a computer know which move to make when the game is too far along (and potentially in an odd configuration) for knowledge about openings to be relevant, but not yet close enough to an endgame for knowledge about closings to be relevant?

I was stunned to learn that few if any researchers had bothered to ask that question. The general answer was that computers consider each possible move, determine how good it is, and pick the best. What does it mean for a midgame move to be "good?" Astoundingly, there was no clear answer. That made it an excellent topic for a doctoral thesis. What made it even better was that there seemed to be a pretty straightforward answer: score each potential move based on the probability that it will lead to a win.

It wasn't exactly rocket science. In fact, it wasn't a remotely new idea. The notion that, on balance, you'd do pretty well for yourself if you maximized expected value is about as basic an idea as you'll find in statistics. To put the matter simply, suppose that, for the same price, you can buy tickets in one of two lotteries. The first lottery pays ten dollars to one out of every ten tickets and zero otherwise, for an expected payout of one dollar. The second lottery pays two dollars on every ticket. The principle of "expected value maximization" says that, on balance, you'd do better in the second lottery. I got an Ivy League PhD for saying, "The same is true in chess." I took a hundred or so pages to say it, though, and I included lots of formulas, tables, and charts, so the Credentialed Elite recognized me as one of their own.

Still, it didn't exactly feel right. I was sure that as soon as I started presenting my work, angry audiences would scream: "That's obvious and trivial! Why are you wasting our time?"

Not what happened. Instead, outraged chess programmers insisted that my work was so counterintuitive that it had to be wrong. They could dismiss it easily without bothering to check the math, the programming, the statistics, the simulations, the results, or the analysis.

I'd touched a nerve. Worse: I'd hit the third rail. Buried within my research was a deeply dangerous implication: the best move to make against an expert player is also the best move to make against a random player. If you've never been in or near the cult of expertise, you probably can't see the danger. To members of the Credentialed Elite, however, the threat is palpable. Their entire self-image and sense of self-worth are bound in their expertise, their prestige, and the adulation of their peers. Here I went ahead and highlighted an area in which there's nothing special about expertise. Expertise might make you adept at explaining what's going on, but it didn't help you make better moves.

I presented my work at a conference, still clueless as to why people couldn't see that everything I was saying was blindingly obvious. There, in the audience, sat none other than Hans Berliner. His star power stole the show. My presentation was supposed to have lasted fifteen minutes. He kept me up there for forty-five, peppering me with questions. The rest of the room fell silent. The leading guru of the computer chess world against a twenty-three-year-old upstart. Finally, he was done. He left the room. As I packed my materials, fully half the room stopped by to commend me on how well I'd handled myself under grueling questioning from a superstar. Not a single person had anything to say about the substance of my work.

I thought back to my casual questioning of Professor Browne. Apparently the rules differ depending upon where you sit in the pecking order. Prestige gets you a free pass from both sound methodology and intellectual consistency. That's true far beyond academia. It's central to understanding modern life, contemporary American institutions, and our new civil war. Everyone likes arguing about results, but the real action is in methodology. If the results—of anything, ever—sound incredibly good, incredibly bad, or just plain incredible, pay more attention to the process that produced them than to the results themselves. That lesson resonates loudly to anyone looking at the 2020 election. If you don't examine methodology, you'll never be able to prove that only the gullible and the willfully blind believe official results that violate common sense.

SUPREMELY ENLIGHTENING

It didn't get any better when I hit law school. At orientation, Dean Andrews took to the stage to explain how important it was to do the reading and participate in class. "Now, I know that some of you may feel self-conscious about participating," he explained sympathetically. "But you don't have to worry. Your class participation won't count in your grade. Your entire grade will be based on your final exam."

My jaw dropped. Wasn't there anyone in Georgetown's Psychology Department who could explain to its esteemed legal faculty that this incentive system was ass backward? Ten years post-PhD, and I still refused to see it. The incentives can't be wrong, by definition. Incentives tell people how to behave, what an institution really is, and who will succeed. If you think they're off, you're in the wrong room. Showing up in law school to engage in spirited exchanges about law, philosophy, and policy meant that I was once again in the wrong room. Dean Andrews was giving us the key to law school success: Impress the impressive professors at the moment they ask you to impress them. Otherwise, stay below the radar.

Two of my classmates taught me how the game was supposed to be played. Dave's goal was to make enough money to support—and spend time with—at least six kids. He scoured the legal world for a niche that was boring, predictable, and necessary. He found one, kept his head down through law school, and shrugged off most of what he saw as nonsense. Last I heard he was a successful ERISA lawyer with a large family. Dave was a man who understood his own priorities, maintained his common sense, invested the money and effort necessary to gain a credential and a skill, and passed largely untouched through an environment that never pretended to speak to him.

Matt, on the other hand, was out to master the art of convincing the right people that he was a good guy to keep around. Matt came to campus at the start of every semester to select his classes. He'd identify professors teaching courses they'd taught many times before, then hit the library where the school shelved previous exams and answer keys. He'd register for courses whose current professors had published the largest collection of relevant answers. Then he'd head out of town, study the answer keys, and come back for finals—in other words, he studied the professors rather than the material. In response to every question, he regurgitated his professor's own work.

Could any impressive law professor fail to be impressed? Within fifteen years, Matt had become a billionaire best known for getting invited into angel rounds at the right startups. An impressive ability to appear impressive, indeed.

The impressive professors I was supposed to impress were indeed a prestigious lot. Many of them had clerked at the Supreme Court. Watching these former clerks taught me a lot about the justices who'd chosen them out of a stellar applicant pool. I had a number of professors who'd clerked for Sandra Day O'Connor. Like the justice herself, they were brilliant people who could survey a situation, spot every detail, ignore those that were truly important, elevate the irrelevant, and reach bizarre conclusions. They brought life to the expression "can't see the forest for the trees."

My favorite case involved a man named Riley. Professor Jayne was particularly proud of her work as the clerk who'd helped Justice O'Connor draft her concurring opinion. I'm not quite sure why she took pride in it, but I suppose that's just part of my overall cluelessness.

Riley was a drug dealer. Big time. Everyone knew it. No one could prove it. The cops stationed themselves outside his house. Riley hadn't made it easy. He'd chosen to live in the Everglades, and he'd built a solid fence around his property. So, the cops got in a helicopter and flew four hundred feet over his house. Then they told a judge that thanks to a couple of broken panes of glass in the roof of Riley's greenhouse, they were able to see marijuana. Based on that probable cause, the judge granted a search warrant. When they searched the house— sure enough—they found more than enough for an easy conviction.

Riley appealed all the way to the Supreme Court. Had the police and judge behaved appropriately? Was the warrant valid? If not, the search of Riley's home was illegal, and all of the evidence discovered in it had to be tossed. The court was split. Four justices said that the applicable question was whether the police had a legal right to fly over Riley's house at four hundred feet. Since they had, the warrant was valid, and the conviction should stand. Four justices said that the applicable question was whether Riley had taken reasonable steps to secure his privacy. Since he had, the warrant and conviction had to be tossed.

Now, it doesn't much matter which of these blocs was asking the right question. What matters is that both blocs answered their respective questions correctly. That is to say, their conclusions followed logically from the questions they asked. While only one of the answers would have helped Riley, either one would have clarified the law. Either answer would have taught future lawyers how to give their clients reasonable advice—which is, at least in theory, what the Supreme Court is supposed to do.

O'Connor, the famed and oddly beloved centrist, split the baby. She adopted one test and the other conclusion. The applicable test is indeed whether Riley had taken reasonable steps to secure his privacy. Clearly, he had not. After all, everyone knows that police helicopters frequently buzz properties at four hundred feet, looking downward. Had Riley really been interested in securing his privacy, he would have ensured that all broken windowpanes in his greenhouse were repaired immediately.

I was stunned. I'm a city boy. What do folks like me do to secure our privacy? Close the door? Throw a deadbolt? Install soundproofing? It dawned upon me that if moving to a swamp, avoiding neighbors, and surrounding your property with an impenetrable fence didn't qualify as reasonable steps to secure your privacy, I'd never met anyone with a reasonable expectation of privacy.

Professor Jayne couldn't see the problem. "I did some work a few years back with military intelligence analysts," I told her. "They showed me some of the technologies they'd used to secure their facilities. Some of them are so expensive they had to get special appropriations from Congress. Is that what it takes?"

"Of course not," she assured me.

"So, suppose I wanted to take reasonable steps to secure my privacy. What would I have to do?"

"Oh, I can't spell it out," she said. "But I think we all know what reasonable steps are."

"OK. Suppose I devise a shielding technology that would cost a million dollars to penetrate. Now, it would be completely unreasonable for anyone to spend that kind of money to overhear my phone calls. Would I have secured my privacy?"

"Yes," she replied.

"OK. Now suppose Bill Gates and Warren Buffet deploy the same technology to secure their phone calls. A million bucks to know what those guys discuss in secret is not a bad investment. Would they have taken reasonable steps to secure their privacy?"

"It doesn't matter who you are. Reasonable steps are reasonable steps."

"OK, but Riley lived in a swamp and built a fence. How is that not a reasonable step to secure his privacy?"

"Read the opinion!" she replied, clearly exasperated.

The problem is, I had.

There's no one more credentialed or more elite than a justice of the Supreme Court. Sometimes it shows. Far too many definitive rulings in America today hinge on the tastes, experiences, and whims of designated experts. Justice O'Connor's idiosyncratic view of privacy—and many other issues, as her jurisprudence shows—may have been more constrained than Saul's plans to fix the world order, but they were just as wacky.

It's getting worse. It used to be considered gauche to suggest that judges elevate their personal worldviews over law, facts, and reason. By the time President Obama got to inject his progressive transformation onto the Supreme Court, however, such personalization had become a qualification. Sonya Sotomayor had famously boasted that as a "wise Latina," her rulings differed from those that a consideration restricted to law and facts might compel. Since becoming a justice, she's proudly deployed her ethnic "wisdom" to promote dissension, division, unequal treatment, and bigotry. Progressive federal judges got the message. They've elevated their personal insights and policy preferences above the determinations of elected officials to issue a flurry of nationwide injunctions.

American jurisprudence, like so much of contemporary culture, is moving outside the Anglo-American tradition, beyond the rule of law, and into the rarefied progressive realm of enlightened elite opinion. Law schools teach their students that there's nothing more impressive than echoing the enlightened views of their elite professors. That was Dean Andrews's orientation message. He was right. Once again, I'd stuck myself in the wrong room.

INSIDE VIEW

You can't really appreciate a cult until it's accepted you as a full member. That's when you learn what it's really about. My first day on USC faculty, the senior-most member of my department popped into my office. Cy was a distinguished scholar. He held a handful of achievement awards, including membership in the National Academy of Engineering. Prestigious. Prominent. A full-fledged member of the Credentialed Elite who knew how to make the system work for him. The previous year, the National Science Foundation had dinged him for misusing federal research funds. Seems he'd classified the guys fixing his roof as research assistants. Or maybe he'd had his research assistants fix his roof. Tough to remember. "If I had to fix the roof myself," he'd said, "I wouldn't have had time to conduct my research." Being distinguished, the NSF asked him not to do it again.

But he wasn't there to warn me about abusing federal funds, or to advise me about how to do it. He wanted to share his wisdom. "You've got six years before you're up for tenure," he said. "Your job is to define an important research direction and to follow it. But I've got to warn you. Watch out for distractions. There are always distractions on campus. The worst distractions are students. They're not here to help you. They're here to waste your time. They get in the way of your research. Whatever you do, don't waste your time on teaching. No one cares about your teaching. It has to be good enough so that parents don't complain to the dean. He hates that. Anything more than that, and you're wasting your time."

I chose to ignore Cy's sage advice. It was a bad move, but I loved teaching. My first teaching assignment was AI: forty students, twelve homework assignments, a midterm, a final, and a term project. Three of the forty did no work. F. F. F.

Dean Clarke knocked on my door. Nothing good could come of that. "One of your students complained about her grade," he said.

"Okay," I said. "Let's take a look at her work." I pulled my files. She'd failed the midterm. Failed the final. Submitted only one homework assignment. Never completed her term project.

The dean reviewed it. "Yes, I certainly agree. This is not a strong performance," he said. "But it looks like she did a nice job on the one assignment she submitted."

"Yes," I said. "I was really impressed with the essay she wrote in response to the question 'Why are you taking this class?' I thought she'd be a great addition to the class discussion. Which she might have been, had she ever shown up."

"No attendance, either?" he asked, sighing.

"Maybe once or twice. Not one of my regulars."

"Well still, one nice essay is something," he said.

"I guess so," I agreed. "But not much."

"Well, do you think it might be enough to earn a D?" he asked.

"Not really," I said. "As far as I can tell, she did no work and learned nothing."

"But she's a black woman," he said. "We don't get many of those in engineering. It would look bad to give her an F."

I took a deep breath. "Doesn't look great that she earned an F. Does it?"

"No, I suppose when you put it that way, it doesn't. But still, we can't make our students study. Or even attend. We can only control the grades we give them."

I got his point. "Tell you what," I said. "Why don't I change all three Fs to Ds? For the sake of consistency—and in fairness to the other students who learned nothing and did no work. And from now on, I won't fail anyone. No one. As long as I'm on faculty, I'll use a D to mean you've learned nothing."

"Sounds like a great solution," he said. "I'm glad to see you're flexible. It's always good to have these talks where I get to know my new faculty."

Dean Clarke was so impressed with my flexibility that he stuck me on the faculty senate. Impressed? Don't be. Faculty senates like to think of themselves as the self-governing internal board of the university. A more accurate description would be a bunch of insiders figuring out how to make their own gigs extra comfortable, and a bunch of window dressing designed to make the sham look broadly participatory and impressively parliamentary. My job was to be a very quiet, very junior part of the window dressing. I blew it.

There was a critical issue on the table. It appears that someone had surveyed our undergrads and determined that a majority of them were insufficiently aware of the diversity of human experience. I wasn't quite sure what that meant, but the data backed it up. There was only one possible remedy: a university-wide diversity requirement.

The floor was open for questions. I waited my turn with the patience befitting a backbencher. "I don't get it. We're an inner-city school. If we're concerned that our students don't appreciate how lucky they are, why don't we show them the neighborhood? Instead of having them read academic articles about poverty statistics, why don't we take them out into the community? Couldn't we work out a program with some local soup kitchens? We could require every undergrad to spend two nights—over four years—volunteering. They'd learn a lot more, and it would be great for our relationship with the community."

The room fell into stunned silence. "Well, that's certainly an interesting idea," said the chair, "but that's not really what we do. We're pretty far along in our discussion of the new diversity requirement. So I think we'll stick with that plan." The action moved on to senators whose questions weren't stupid.

The next day, Vice Provost Manley spotted me walking across campus. That's even worse than having a dean approach. "I hear you created quite a stir at the faculty senate," she said.

"Not really," I said. "I just think that this whole new requirement is overkill. There are better ways to sensitize our students. I don't really get what we think we're trying to accomplish."

She laughed. "I think you're missing the point. Enrollment in the Sociology Department has been way down for the past couple of years. Our ethnic and gender studies programs are suffering even worse. Sending kids to soup kitchens wouldn't accomplish anything."

My heresies ran deeper. I won an award for innovative teaching. Nothing kills an academic career faster than a teaching award. Good teachers threaten the system. They risk raising the standards. No one—absolutely no one—wants that. Students protesting apartheid is one thing. Any decent university can roll with that. But the thought of students protesting low teaching standards? Another matter entirely. If the students ever figured out how little they get for their tuition dollars, the whole scheme could implode. Teaching awards suggest a faculty member who's forgotten the key to academic success: whatever you do, don't let the students know that competent teaching is possible!

Innovative teaching awards also have the tendency to get you on the committee that evaluates the following year's innovative teaching proposals. Twenty professors from around the university submitted proposals. We had funding for six awards. Dean Kane sent around the proposals prior to our meeting. Three proposals stood out from the crowd. Everyone on the committee saw it. All five of us agreed on the top three. Then one of the other members spoke up: "I can't help but notice that we've given three awards to men. The next one should go to a woman," she said.

I was stunned. "Excuse me?" I asked. "I can't be part of a committee that balances merit against demographics. That's just offensive. It's sexist. If you'd like to cordon off part of the budget to create an award for which only women are eligible, I'll support you. Then our female faculty members will have two shots at awards, while the men will only have one. But there's no way I'm going to figure in the gender of the proposer when evaluating merit."

Silence. Allies? None evident. Dean Kane broke it. "Well, I suppose we shouldn't change the criteria in the middle of the process. We should evaluate the remaining proposals on the merits."

So we did. Strictly on the merits. When the dust settled, we gave three awards to men and three to women. Had they gone with my ranking, it would have been four and two. The real irony? Neither of the women who should have won made the committee's cut. They'd mistakenly addressed topics of general interest rather than those of interest to women. Apparently when you weigh gender against merit, you also redefine merit. Poorly. That's far from a minor problem. It goes straight to the heart of the vaunted meritocracy justifying so much of contemporary reality. A meritocracy is only as good as those who define merit allow it to be.

Then there were faculty meetings.

There was the time that Dean Clarke asked for volunteers to speak about our research to incoming freshmen. I signed up. Sounded like a great idea. To me. Alone. Selected comments from my colleagues included: "I don't really like discussing my research with people who aren't at my level." "That might work in some departments, but what we do here is just too technical to explain to freshmen." "There couldn't be seven people on the planet who could understand my last paper." That last one was asserted as a particular point of pride. It hit me hard. It was completely antithetical my own values.

I cared deeply about opening the minds of students and advancing the frontiers of scientific understanding. I was pushing that agenda in an institution dedicated to smug self-satisfaction, mutual admiration, and personal comfort. Academia was far from what it claimed to be. I began to wonder whether the very idea of an institution committed to education and research was pure fantasy. Was I in the wrong place? Did the right place exist? Was there any American institution that shared my values?

FOLLOW THE SCIENCE

Those questions resonated loudly. The evidence kept on mounting. There was the year that our department chair saw an impressive demo from the AI Learning Lab at the University of Illinois. A large part of the lab was focused on learning by analogy: teach the computer one scientific principle and watch it infer an analogous one. That year, by sheer coincidence, out of hundreds of faculty applicants, the five we interviewed all came from the Illinois Learning Lab. Their work was slick. They presented it well. They seemed like nice guys.

Their training, however, struck me as a bit parochial. One of them had a slide, headed "History of Analogical Reasoning," showing the evolution of work leading to his dissertation. It included his own thesis advisor, his advisor's advisor, a second member of his thesis committee, and that professor's advisor. It was a rather abbreviated view of history. I asked him if he'd looked at any of the earlier work on analogical reasoning. He seemed perplexed. I suggested perhaps starting with Aristotle and filling in the gaps to Dewey. He smiled. Everyone in the room laughed. "Sure," he explained. "Plenty of people have used the same keywords in the past. But nothing anyone came up with before computers could be relevant. If it's from more than ten years ago, it's not worth studying."

I was appalled. I was also the outlier. His eagerness to ignore all but the very recent was standard. I looked around the room. No one else seemed to notice he'd embarrassed himself. My colleagues looked pleased that he'd put me in my place. By that time, I'd developed a reputation for asking silly questions. The belief that those who came before us simply operated at lower planes of intellectual or moral planes permeates the university. Today, a progressive movement called #DisruptTexts disdains everything written from the dawn of time to the 1950s as reflecting a discredited, unevolved ethos.

Our applicant moved on to the content of his work. He outlined some experiments he'd run teaching simple physics to the machine. He taught his AI system that if you have two beakers of water, one containing a great deal and one containing far less, and you open a channel so that the water can all flow together, both beakers would end up at the same level. He then asked it what would happen if he dropped a hot stone into cold water. The program inferred that the water and stone would end up at the same temperature. It was an impressive display.

"What if," I asked, "you dropped a red stone into blue water. Would your system infer that they'd both end up the same color?"

He looked perplexed. "No," he said. "Of course not."

"Why not?" I asked.

"Because they wouldn't end up the same color," he responded. "There's no physical principle of conservation of color." He was a perfect fit for the department. I was not.

It was hardly just my department. The whole university seemed to operate under a value system I couldn't really grasp. I collaborated with some friends at the university's Institute for Safety and Systems Management (ISSM). ISSM was an interesting place. Back in the 1960s, USC had brought in a founding director to build an institute like no other. He did. He hired some world-class researchers, told them they could live anywhere they wanted, and had them teach courses on military bases around the country. That strategy turned ISSM into a cash cow. Not only did the university charge full tuition dollars while offloading overhead onto the military, those courses helped build great connections with rising young officers on their way to positions in which they got to sign contracts and disburse money.

It was brilliant. It was lucrative. The administration hated it. It made them feel like a correspondence school. It wasn't the sort of thing Stanford would do. Or Harvard. Or Yale. Or MIT. Far from impressing the impressive people USC most wanted to impress, ISSM became a source of shame. So, they cut off the military connection, broke ties with alumni who wanted to fund campus research, turned it into a money pit, and watched many of the prestigious hires leave. Then they complained that ISSM research was subpar and that it was losing money.

It all contributed to this sinking feeling that I wasn't going to make it, that my cult would soon decide that it had no room for the likes of me. Academia is no place for an intellectually curious, broadly interested, multidisciplinary, collaborative, genuinely egalitarian, committed teacher.

I was far more than a teacher, though. Cy had been right. It was all about research. The ability to break new ground and then convince your friends that it was ground worth breaking is central to the Credentialed Elite's self-image. Chess and the other games I'd studied on my way to my doctorate were a starting point, but the luminaries of AI wanted to see something different.

My thesis work fell into a niche called "heuristic search." In late-1980s AI, search was passé. As more than one senior AI type reminded me, search had seemed interesting back in the '70s, but the field had run its course. There was nothing interesting left to say about search algorithms. It was the sort of spectacularly backward error that only the Credentialed Elite can make, that the Credentialed Elite make often, and for which no member of the Credentialed Elite has ever suffered.

There's only so much you can do when your field has gone hopelessly awry. I defined some questions of broader interest: How does the ability to collect and manipulate information quickly and easily make the world a better place? How does it help individuals make better decisions, organizations devise better strategies, and governments adopt better policies? Then I chose a direction: I plunged into the esoteric world of probabilistic and statistical approaches to decision-making under uncertainty in AI systems.

It felt like a winner. I mean, it had to be a winner. Computers do one thing: they compute. Ask any question. If you can translate it into a computational problem, a computer can help you. If not, you're out of luck. So basically, computers like math. And math has right answers. Tell a computer what inputs to plug into a mathematical equation, and it will give you the right answers.

AI systems try to answer questions when you don't know all the inputs. That means you have to make some guesses. AI systems require you to make choices while you lack certainty. Make good choices, and an AI system will make good recommendations. Make bad choices, and you're out of luck. Kind of like life.

Now, probability is the mathematical field that translates doubts and guesses into numbers. So probability had to be the way to build AI systems. Obvious, right? Not to the experts. To the Credentialed Elite then governing AI, probabilistic approaches were off limits—even less relevant than search algorithms. Daniel Bobrow, then editor-in-chief of the preeminent AI journal, even returned one of my articles unreviewed. His brief cover letter explained, "Your paper is primarily mathematical and therefore not of interest to our readership." It all made sense inside the cult—and the cult's incentives were rigged to keep it making sense.

How had the cultists reached such an obviously absurd point? Through the concerted efforts of luminaries so credentialed and so elite that they put Berliner to shame. Twenty or so years earlier,

Patrick Hayes and John McCarthy—the heads of the MIT and Stanford AI programs, respectively—had published a paper "proving" that probability was incapable of capturing the sort of knowledge AI systems needed. No, AI required inventing whole new theories that didn't give you right answers. Why? To capture the mathematics of screwups. After all, humans screw up. Why shouldn't computers? Probability theory might lead to systems that make good recommendations, maybe even better recommendations than people. Who wants computers to be better than people? AI is supposed to be "artificial intelligence." Intelligence involves screwups.

Scratch the surface, and what do you know? That was just the cover story. They needed it to sound good. The real story was cleverer by far. After all, these folks were among the finest gurus America's cult of expertise had to offer. Cleverness in the cause of gilding the cult's cages was what they did best.

Back around the same time they proved that good math couldn't work for AI, they convinced the federal government to sink a lot of money into AI. The government built ultra-cool AI labs for AI researchers. But the gurus were afraid that the government might want something back—maybe start making noise about return on investment, or results, or some such nonsense. What to do? Convince the government that short-term results were impossible. Only long-term basic research was worthwhile. In fact, even measurable progress was impossible. AI's luminaries convinced the feds to sink a ton of money into research labs, where they could do whatever they wanted as long as they deemed their own results "interesting."

To make it work, though, they had to ensure that none of the AI researchers availing themselves of that ample funding crossed them up by producing results. If anyone started turning out results, the feds would know that results were possible. They might demand that other people produce results as well. And things like results or measurable progress were deadly to the system—even worse than showing students that competent teaching is possible. What to do? Insist that everyone look in silly places, in a direction that no useful result might ever be found. Cut off anyone trying to do something that might make sense.

It was a great scam. Golden. The best thing about it? The folks behind it probably didn't even know it was a scam—or even a plan. In their world, given the incentives before them, it all just kind of flowed together. Impressed? Now you should be. There's a reason luminaries get to be luminaries. It's also a stark reminder that there are excellent reasons for forcing freshmen to check their common sense at the university gates.

I never had a chance. I was a headstrong whiz kid who believed the mythology. By the time I showed up on the AI scene, everyone in AI knew that search algorithms and probabilistic systems were for losers. Yet there I was, pushing search algorithms and probabilistic systems just because they made sense. Loser. That was roughly thirty years ago. These days, when AI systems actually produce results, they're all based in probability and statistics. By the time AI got there, however, I'd moved on.

The rules of the Credentialed Elite are clear: Those who've been embraced and promoted are always right, even when they're provably wrong. Those who've been rejected must forever be wrong, even when they can prove they'd been right. When the entire system is based upon impressing your colleagues, it's poor form to notice that your colleagues are entirely devoid of common sense. Those who do so are clearly refusing to "follow the science."

Those rules govern contemporary American society far beyond the hallowed halls of academia. They're the basis of the entrenched government bureaucracy that forms America's permanent Deep State.

3

THE LONG MARCH

INCREMENTAL OUTRAGEOUSNESS

The groundwork for twenty-first-century progressivism was laid decades ago. It's a strategy Marxist radicals devised in the 1960s: the long march through America's institutions. Now that they've spent decades marching, their cult of expertise has corrupted every important institution in America. It's done so by corrupting the incentive systems that determine success. As young people enter our elite institutions, they behave the way those incentives motivate them to behave. From there, the debasement of the institution follows as a matter of course.

Progressivism has become a broad-based cultural phenomenon. It's not the product of a select few. There's no puppeteer. The Soros, Clinton, and Obama networks, the Rockefeller and Tides foundations, many UN agencies, numerous nonprofits, various international organizations, and select Davos grandees may be significant contributors to the problem, but they didn't create progressivism, and they don't control it. They're superelites with enormous resources, talent, cynicism, and corrupt values who've glommed onto a cruelly destructive system and made it work for them. Their leaders are self-interested, self-important elitist oligarchs—not masters of the universe.

Progressivism is organic. It arose through the interactions of hundreds, then thousands, then millions, now hundreds of millions of people making rational decisions given the incentives they were handed—and that they then internalized. Those internalized incentives gave birth to a moral code deeply at odds with Judeo-Christian ethics and America's founding ideals. To restore America, we must first understand, then alter, the incentives that feed progressivism. We began on campus because those incentives and their corrupting effect began on campus.

Tales of campus outrage far more egregious than my own adventures have become legendary. There are entire organizations committed to tracking them, and they can't keep up with the pace of outrage. What's not understood, however, is that the reworking of academia in the mid-twentieth century guaranteed that our universities would become dangerously detached from reality. That guarantee was in place long before it was possible to see the specifics of the detachment. What guaranteed it was an incentive system that enforced orthodox thinking: incremental outrageousness.

The accelerated pace of campus outrages over the past decade illustrates the relationship between the progressive oligarchs and progressives in the field. Offenses were already proliferating at a frightening pace when the Obama Department of Education announced that it would penalize any university that provided due process to students accused of offending progressive sensibilities. In other words, oligarchical government progressives motivated elite campus progressives to drop whatever constraints bourgeoise morality or constitutionalism might have placed in their way. Campus progressives were thrilled to comply.

That episode demonstrated clearly how progressivism grows through seduction, not manipulation. The difference is critical. Seduction grants people license to do what they want to do; it frees them from external constraints to pursue their true desires. Manipulation tricks people into doing things they don't want to do. Progressives manipulate plenty, but their greatest advances have arisen through seduction.

Thanks to incremental outrageousness, no one ever needed to conspire to inflict progressivism on America—or the West. Seduction was far easier, far more pleasurable, and far more lucrative to the elite. Progressive leaders simply encourage people to jettison the constraints of traditional morality in favor of those of the progressive morality they learned to internalize on campus.

The inner workings of American academia are not hard to discern. A small number of recognized luminaries announce "important directions" for their fields of study. Those directions come to define orthodox thinking for the field. Each participant must then move a little bit further in the designated direction. The "little bit" contributes to a foundation on which others can build. The "further" enhances the reputation of those who built the foundation upon which it stands. The "designated direction" ensures that the luminaries remain in charge.

Because the predecessors who contributed to that foundation make all decisions about who succeeds and who fails, the surest path to success is to flatter the senior people in your field. The surest way to flatter them is by moving their own work a little bit further along the approved path—meaning a little bit further from the initial observation that first motivated movement in that direction. Voila! Incremental outrageousness.

This incentive system guarantees that every academic field will move slightly further from reality with each new "discovery," unless and until reality forces it to recalibrate—what economists call a market correction. Over time, each discipline becomes increasingly detached from the real world. As that happens, faculties become increasingly defensive. They have no choice but to become increasingly insular and intolerant of disapproved thoughts. If reality were ever to intrude, their entire ego-driven self-images would come tumbling down.

That guaranteed flight from reality rings true for every single academic discipline, from engineering and medicine to literature and sociology. What differs across fields is how often reality intrudes in a manner so obvious that even those most devoted to orthodox thinking must recalibrate. When that happens, the field moves en masse, maintaining all existing pecking orders, to insist that its previous orthodoxy hadn't really led it down an embarrassing path of wasted time and resources; instead, it provided critical information necessary to discover the new truth to which all must now adhere. In scientific and professional fields, these sorts of market corrections may intrude once a decade; in social sciences and humanities, perhaps once a century.

The most recent redirections in the social sciences and humanities occurred in the quarter century or so following the end of World War II. That's not surprising. If the events that roiled Western civilization between 1914 and 1945 don't qualify as intrusions of reality so great that no one can ignore them, nothing does. In those postwar decades, most luminaries in the social sciences and humanities leaned toward the left, on a spectrum from committed New Dealers to hard-core communists and black separatists. They provided the new directions for their fields. For decades, every "advance" in those fields moved one step further to the left, and one step further away from reality. The result is the contemporary leftist movement called progressivism—which did not gel into its present form until the early twenty-first century.

Progressivism was born and raised amid this incentive system. Over the years, the progressive view of justice and equity drifted further from anything that any other ethical system might recognize as justice and equity. Its notions of race, gender, freedom, rights, and America drifted just as far from reality to become increasingly outrageous. The drift was so incremental for so long that it was often hard to spot. Once people checked in and suspended their common sense in the name of "higher learning," the path seemed logical. Incremental outrageousness was in; common sense was out.

Incremental outrageousness does more than just reward fabulists. It shapes the way that we see reality. Behavior—yours, mine, America's, the world's—emerges entirely from perception. Sure, it's nice when our perceptions match reality, but anyone who's ever driven over a curb has experienced a gap between perception and reality. The closer our perceptions are to reality, the more successful we're likely to be. That's true in our personal lives as well as in the lives of nations. Incremental outrageousness drives perceptions further and further from reality with each passing step. Thanks to incremental outrageousness, the academic universe has become increasingly illusory.

Decades into the long march, America has fallen into that progressive illusion. The progressivism that dominates and defines contemporary American culture is dangerously divorced from reality. It rejects basic biology, essential human nature, and social constructs forged through millennia of painful experience. It clings to its rejections tightly, refusing to recognize clear facts and railing against inconvenient theories capable of explaining reality. As a result, it's also tremendously underconfident, exploding in unreasoning rage at anyone who dares to question its foundational beliefs. Most importantly, it's fighting hard to transform America into something consistent with its own utopian fantasies—fantasies that may make sense in the illusion but would prove deadly in reality.

Progressive fantasies became particularly dangerous when they graduated and moved off campus. Graduates returning home and entering the workplace brought their progressive indoctrination with them. That inflicted considerable damage on key industries like media and the government—neither of which enjoy or deserve public trust, and both of which are demonstrably lacking in integrity.

Even more deadly, the progressive cultists convinced ordinary people to "trust the experts." Academics have a monopoly on credentialing experts. Trusting the expert on questions related to social sciences and humanities, including topics like social policy, government organization, the meaning of justice, and basic ethics, meant that academic progressivism became the ideology of trusted experts. Everything else, including traditional American values and Judeo-Christian morality, became the ideology of uneducated reactionaries terrified of advancement, change, and "science."

Millions accepted expert nonsense because the cult's calling card seemed so compelling: Trust the experts! After all, if you can't trust the people who've dedicated their lives to the study of history, or literature, or law, or public health, or engineering to know the truth about history, literature, law, public health, and engineering, whom can you trust?

America was unwise to trust the experts. Experts are not particularly trustworthy on anything other than narrow, technical matters. Experts are far more committed to their own interests than to the interests of the public at large. Experts push ideas, theories, and policies that serve the interests of the scientific establishment and their own careers rather than the cause of science—or the public interest. Trusting the experts led to an unprecedented bifurcation of American society into the very successful and very credentialed on the one hand, and those who spend every day hoping to survive on the other. Trusting the experts is what impeded the social and economic mobility that long made America exceptional and great. Trusting the experts is what got us the gross inequality that characterizes contemporary American society. America's commitment to trusting the experts has been very good for the experts. It's been very bad for America. Surprise!

Then things got worse. Social media—available to anyone—turned incremental outrageousness into society's dominant incentive system. On any issue, at any time, the biggest prizes go to those who most successfully combine elements of truth with elements of outrageousness. Those hewing too close to the truth are bland; those who are exclusively outrageous are too easily dismissed. As with academia before it, the sweet spot belongs to those who can be incrementally more outrageous than the most recent champion. With social media, the pace accelerated. The outrages still move incrementally, but the steps are faster than ever. Objective reality is no longer even within view of the progressive vanguard. Escape velocity is within reach.

The stars aligned perfectly for progressivism—and dangerously for America. The bizarre stories emanating from campus are merely signs that it exists in a parallel universe, a world of illusion and fantasy. Graduates who've gone through the entire system after its divorce from reality seeded the country with progressive poison. Social media elevated outrageousness into an art form. When a young, exciting, charismatic, ethnically suitable, progressive leader arose preaching hope and change, progressivism tightened its hold on American culture and took it on an accelerating ride into oblivion.

President Obama entered office promising a progressive transformation. That's precisely what he delivered. He did not, however, have time to finish the job. In 2016, he passed the mantle to a resistance movement committed to fighting the restoration of America's founding values and principles. The outrages moved forward at a frightening pace.

The statues felled during the summer of 2020 highlight a terrifying truth: the cult of expertise is on the verge of becoming a full-blown faith. Like all new faiths, it's moving to dismantle the iconography of the old order. We are witnessing—and living with—the predictable results of a dismal system. Plenty of people have identified its outrages. Relatively few have focused on its internal workings—the incentives that motivate people to convert decent intentions into outrageous behavior. That's both tragic and strategically disastrous. It's why the American republic is now in need of restoration.

HARD-LEARNED LESSONS

Actual outrages are but symptoms of an underlying disease. To defeat progressivism, we must expose the academic disease that caused those outrages. My own academic story is a tiny part of that exposé. Telling it means I have to swallow an uncomfortable truth: I was not a successful academic. Nor, for that matter, was I a particularly good one. I tried—or at least, I thought I was trying. I conducted pioneering research. I published widely. I was a committed teacher. I engaged in student life. I even served on more than my share of committees.

Wrong! Those are all things that appear in the job description. Those are also areas into which at least some successful academics pour considerable effort—and may even place some value. They are not, however, what academia is about. Nor are they the skills required to succeed in academia. In fact, they're completely at odds with the incentives and values driving academic success. Academia is—first, last, and entirely—a mutual admiration society. You might even say . . . a cult.

The senior members of any faculty have friends, colleagues, and distant luminaries they want to impress. When it came time for me to go up for tenure, the question was simple: Had I impressed the AI luminaries my senior colleagues wanted me to impress? It was a trick question. Relatively few of the folks I was supposed to impress impressed me; those who conceded that they knew who I was (junior people, after all, are largely beneath their notice) returned the favor. They deemed my work "peripheral." Given where they wanted to take the field, they were right. The prestigious academics whose work I found impressive—and who returned that favor—were not computer scientists researching AI. They were in fields actually interested in human behavior, strategy formation, and decision-making—fields like cognitive psychology and behavioral economics. Impressing the wrong people didn't score me any points. It just proved that I'd been operating within the wrong incentive system.

Once again, though, I'm not sharing my story because it was particularly egregious. I'm sharing it because it was representative. In fact, it was likely far smoother than it would have been had I chosen a path through the humanities or the social sciences. To the extent that objectivity and rationality find any place on campus, it's the engineering school—and it's in pathetically short supply there.

The commitment to orthodoxy and the fear of challenging ideas is baked into the academic incentive system. Success flows most easily to those who can push the conventional wisdom of their fields one half step further in whatever direction it's already moving—incremental outrageousness. If people can get ideological, partisan, nasty, and defensive about computer chess, could you expect anything less when it comes to the study of poverty or the environment?

My journey from whiz kid to exiled renegade taught me a lot about academia, the Credentialed Elite, and the cult of expertise. Our universities have become bizarre combinations of subjectivity and indoctrination. Professors define their own truths and their own values. Only fidelity to the orthodoxy matters. Students who question the professor's truth risk severe penalties. The student's own beliefs and values are irrelevant.

How did we get here? The key is faculty governance. It creates the ultimate insider/outsider problem. What do faculty members get to decide? Hiring, firing, and promotion of junior colleagues. Curriculum design. The articles published in prestigious journals. The appropriate paths for research in their fields. The availability of public and private research funding.

Academia exists without near-term market criteria—often by design, as I discovered during my years in AI. The only thing that matters is peer approval. Can you impress your friends? Congratulations! You must be very good at what you do, whatever that is. And never forget: the key to impressing your friends is telling them how impressive their work is. In academia today, the Credentialed Elite devise impressive theories untethered to reality. They assert them with moral certainty. They deride those who question their brilliance. The lunatics run the asylum. The very structure of American academia renders it irrelevant at best, most likely dangerous. Incremental outrageousness in action.

As bad as things were in computer science—and they were bad—they were far worse in the social sciences and the humanities. At least in engineering and business, reality intrudes occasionally. Professional and technical programs can only remain on silly tangents for so long before reality snaps them back. Of course, none of the folks who pushed the tangent ever admit they were wrong, and none of the folks who throw funding at them ever admit they'd funded the wrong researchers, but at least reality clubs them over the head once a decade or so.

Even AI caved to reality—though not until my work been indelibly labeled peripheral. Some luminaries eventually decided that probability was useful after all. As is always the case, the implication that they'd been publishing the wrong work and promoting the wrong people for decades had zero effect on their positions or prestige. I might have been right about the science, but I'd been dead wrong about the scientific establishment.

In fact, it appears that I might have been *very* right about the science. Amid the numerous improbabilities of 2020 was a contact I received from some Australian podcasters excited to have tracked me down. Seems that my quaint notion of using big data and simulation in AI was decades ahead of its time—and suddenly getting cited widely. I laughed. "Live long enough," I told them. Then I had to explain why. My research may have been prescient, but I was still a failure as an academic.

The less quantitative a field, the worse the flight from reality. Social science and humanities tangents can last for decades. Those fields just get sillier and sillier, more and more bizarre. World Order with Saul probably qualifies as middling these days. Most of those programs don't even pretend anymore. They're propaganda shops, out to indoctrinate a new batch of young people into the Progressive Gospel of the Credentialed Elite. Social science and humanities departments are the most cultlike parts of the cult of expertise, which is why it's hardly surprising that more than any other American institutions, they're responsible for progressivism and the threat it poses to America.

It's structural bias in action. That decades-ago first step chose the direction. The incentive system guaranteed its divergence from reality. Where else could incremental outrageousness lead? Tenure, faculty governance, and peer review create a central-planning mentality. Central planning is a guaranteed loser—even if you hire the very best central planners. Take it from a CS guy: changing your inputs may change your outputs, but if your internal rules remain intact, you'll never solve your problem.

Academic orthodoxy provides the inputs. Academic incentives process them. The output is toxic. It's destroying America. And it's endemic. We'll never restore America's founding values until we rework the incentive structure of academia.

I saw it. I was too naïve to hide that I could see it. That made me dangerous. By the mid-1990s, I found myself wondering how long it would be before people realized that our finest institutions are hollow shells that do nothing well. Maybe branding. Maybe. Other than that? They're bad at teaching. Their research is only as good as the leading Credentialed Elite let it be. Every now and then a pocket of genuine world-class excellence manages to flourish, but such pockets are far fewer and much further between than anyone seeking a reasonable return on our national investment should demand. The people are clueless. They shut out common sense. They shut down questioning. They lie to themselves. They lie to others. They hold those they consider their inferiors in contempt. They're terribly inefficient. The entire edifice is a façade.

The Credentialed Elite defining orthodoxies shut down scientific inquiry to game their funding. Results that threaten those orthodoxies are dismissed, condemned, defamed. The vaunted peer-review process does a decent job at finding the best examples of orthodox thinking, but hand it a paper at odds with the orthodoxy, and the peers kill it on principle. Then the Credentialed Elite deride it because their own publications rejected it. The whole thing is a joke, an exercise in self-aggrandizement, a mutual admiration society. Want to find the best examples of thinking consistent with the orthodoxy? The top academic journals are a fine place to look. Want to find interesting ideas that might break a logjam in the orthodoxy? Avoid anything the Credentialed Elite considers prestigious. Great ideas are out there, on the periphery: among the sidelined members of the Credentialed Elite, among those too productive to worry about credentials, and among those who've retained their common sense. Once again, meritocracy can never be better than those who define merit. Never confuse the finest contributions to orthodox thinking with the finest contributions to society—or science.

It gets worse. Tuition has risen at triple the rate of inflation—for decades! There are now more administrators than faculty members, nationwide. Universities have been bilking America's taxpayers like there's no tomorrow. They take research dollars while ensuring that useful results rarely emerge. They take tuition dollars while minimizing teaching. They take federally guaranteed student loans without providing marketable skills. They call themselves nonprofits, avoid taxation, amass endowments in the billions, turn themselves into hedge funds, and become activist investors. Then they impose their progressive notions about victimhood and entitlement on corporate America.

Renegades like me may be a clear and present danger to academia, but academia has become a clear and present danger to America.

THE GRADUATE

Let's leave campus. Lord knows, I did. Let's look at the pathological progeny the cult of expertise unleashed upon an unprepared America: progressivism.

We hear the word all the time, but how often do we try to understand what it is or how it took over our country? It's worth a bit of time to contemplate the birth and growth of the movement that threatens to bring down America.

In the years following World War II, the luminaries of numerous academic disciplines asked important, bold, compelling questions: Should we pay more attention to the conquered when we study history? Have we underplayed the roles of racial or religious bigotry in attempting to understand society? Have we systematically ignored wonderful works of art, literature, and music because women, minorities, or non-Western cultures produced them? These and comparably intriguing questions set new directions for the humanities and the social sciences.

From those intellectually credible beginnings, the redirected disciplines took on lives of their own. Every incentive impelled each Newly Credentialed down the slippery slope of incremental outrageousness toward inevitable absurdity. Academic departments are self-replicating by design. Absolutely every incentive in academia promotes orthodox thinking. That's doubly true in the humanities and social sciences, where objective validation is nearly impossible, and reality rarely intrudes.

Teachers spew the rigid orthodoxy of their fields while deriding those who might question it. Undergrads are expected to absorb orthodoxy as accepted wisdom. If I'd learned that lesson when Saul tried to teach it to me, I might be the Messiah today (probably not)— or at the very least, I might have been a successful academic. Periodically, recognized luminaries—like Hayes and McCarthy in AI— designate new directions of inquiry capable of ensuring that nothing of value can emerge. Once their edict has come down from on high, the path is set. Each new generation of graduate students must push the field further from reality along the designated tangent. All are prohibited from mentioning shifts to orthodoxy; today's truth has always been accepted truth, even if it was taught as false yesterday. I learned that from Berliner. Others might recognize it from Orwell.

In the 1960s, the military draft shifted the system into overdrive. Students attending college and graduate school were able to get deferments far more easily than those who were not. Universities opened their doors wide to accept any student with any aptitude who wished to pursue a graduate degree. In the hard sciences, engineering, law, medicine, mathematics, statistics, economics, and finance, external forces contributed to maintaining at least some semblance of standards. In the humanities, arts, and less mathematical social sciences, the nation's collective tenured faculty was free to set any standards it deemed fit. Understanding that the larger the department, the more money and clout it enjoys, the faculties of those disciplines carefully set standards low enough that nearly anyone interested could meet them.

The system kicked into high gear. Competition for positions swelled. Overall competence declined precipitously. The grad student population leaned heavily toward the antiwar left—often buying into the entire anti-American New Left agenda. Rewards flowed to the most sycophantic new entrants capable of producing the most outrageous work. Entire disciplines ran hard and fast away from reality. By the 1980s, these marginally competent radical extremists were represented heavily in the tenured ranks. By 2000, they were firmly in control.

Once these miseducated, narrowminded, underconfident egotists came to dominate the Credentialed Elite, the game was over. They all but eliminated the Western canon, denigrated American history and the nation's founding ideals, required identity indoctrination courses for all undergraduates, shouted down competing ideas and curious questions, and rendered it nearly impossible to obtain a liberal arts education in the United States. In its place, they glorified grievance and victimhood. Any student who arrived with any sort of baggage was taught to celebrate it, bask in it, claim it as a badge of moral superiority. Universities effectively granted such students licenses to impose pain on any and all who reminded them of the individuals or groups on whom they blamed their emotional baggage.

To help it along, universities also pioneered previously unimagined frontiers in inefficiency. A million administrators bloomed. The labor surplus fed a system of adjunct teachers, often far superior to their tenured colleagues as educators, but paid a pittance and treated with contempt.

With the help of government bureaucrats and a massive PR machine, tuition skyrocketed. Guaranteed student loans ensured that all could attend; few felt the sting of debt until after graduation. By that time, the institution that had bilked them was out of the picture: "Wait! You mean you thought that your marginally passing grades as a gender studies major at a third-tier university would let you repay a six-figure student debt before you hit twenty-five? Wow! We can only apologize for the misunderstanding. No refunds! But perhaps you'd like some advice about protesting the bank holding the note?"

Universities are by far the least accountable corporations in America.

No matter how poor the product, no matter how misleading the advertising, no matter how outrageous the cost, their immunity from product liability is total. Life really is good for the Credentialed Elite.

By the early twenty-first century, however, good was hardly enough. The fall of the Soviet Union had shattered the Western left. Perhaps the primary reason the 1990s were such a prosperous decade is that there was no functioning hard left; the centrism of Bill Clinton and Tony Blair was as far left as the West would go. In the space of a few years around 2000, however, a number of events converged to reinvigorate the Left and give form to twenty-first century progressivism.

The Seattle WTO Riots of 1999 cemented progressive economics in the Marxist tradition, a worthy successor to the defeated Soviet communism. The presidential election of 2000 freed progressivism from any affinity its advocates may once have felt for the US Constitution, its federal structure, and its Bill of Rights. The UN's Durban Conference of 2001 enshrined progressivism as the newest in a long line of ideologies committed to destroying the Jews. The 9/11 attacks impelled progressivism to ally itself with the violent supremacists preaching Islamism and jihad. The 1999 introduction of the Euro and China's 2001 accession to the WTO served as catalysts.

Progressivism graduated. It moved off campus into society at large. It emerged as a twenty-first-century anticapitalist, antisemitic, authoritarian Western movement allied with Islamism. Its ancestors—the various failed variants of Marxism that had immiserated so many in the twentieth century—beamed with pride at their worthy successor.

INTO THE WORKFORCE

While universities were the birthplace of progressivism, other industries proved nearly as susceptible. Back about the time that the

Vietnam War was skewing the ideological makeup of the Newly Cre-dentialed, academia picked up its most important ally: the media.

Watergate, and specifically the role of Woodward, Bernstein, and the *Washington Post*, infected American journalism with a deadly virus. With the help of their glorification in Hollywood's *All the Pres-ident's Men*, Woodward and Bernstein motivated two generations of journalists to make news rather than report it.

Graduates heading toward careers in journalism enter the pro-fession committed to shaping public opinion for "the good." What defines the good? Progressive morality, of course—as these budding new activists-cum-journalists learned on campus. The result has been the debasement of journalism—the replacement of reporting with fake news, an end to objectivity, and (more recently) suppression of important news items running counter to the progressive narrative.

Media progressivism picks up right where academic progressivism leaves off. Academics give progressive gibberish the patina of exper-tise; media trumpet it widely to an audience untrained in spotting academic nonsense. At least in the Soviet Union, readers understood that *Pravda* spouted lies and propaganda; a stunning number of Americans still believe what they read in the *New York Times* and the *Washington Post*.

Journalism was hardly the last stop of the progressive juggernaut. The deeply indoctrinated Gen Xers and millennials in the workforce knew nothing else. To them, "being a progressive" was synonymous with "being a decent person." They inflicted campus progressivism upon society at large. They took over Hollywood and the tech sector. They made significant inroads into finance and law. They came to dominate the civil service.

Then all hell broke loose. Social media shot the academic incentive structure across America. That's why it's so important to understand the incentives driving academia. Only a deep understanding of academic incentives can explain why progressivism grows more extreme, more absurd, more demanding, and further detached from reality with each passing year. Incremental outrageousness has become the defining feature of the twenty-first century.

With the advent of social media, the pace of the progressive transformation reached dizzying speeds. Rewards flowed exclusively to the most extreme, the most outrageous, the most aggrieved. Whereas in earlier times the gauntlet of graduate school weeded out all but the most committed, social media democratized the flight from reality—and from personal responsibility. All of a sudden, anyone with a bizarre and outrageous theory could shape public discourse. It was a glorious dawn for conspiracy theorists, as evidence-free progressive notions like apocalyptic climate change and implicit, undetectable systemic racism assumed national and global significance.

Academia provided more than merely the incentive system driving progressive social media dominance. It also provided the theoretical glue necessary to turn a mob of pathetic, navel-gazing, self-entitled victims into a formidable progressive army. Intersectionality bound them all together: Anyone fighting in one progressively approved struggle was required to subscribe to the entire progressive agenda. Anything less made them part of the problem, complicit in the structural injustice progressives everywhere sought to dismantle. Microaggressions ensured that any member of any authorized group could quickly assemble a lifetime of grievances.

Social media proved to be the final piece progressivism needed to conquer American culture. Perhaps more than anything else, progressivism had spent its college years preparing for a career in politics. The shattering of the Left with the fall of the Soviet Union had created an opening for a new aristocratic leftism of the Credentialed

Elite. Though it drew upon odious ideas of the past, it was not until the dawn of the twenty-first century that a full-fledged Credentialed Elite progressivism was poised to emerge.

Throughout the 1990s, Bill Clinton had triangulated to sit between House Speaker Republican Newt Gingrich and Minority Leader Democrat Dick Gephardt. That positioning led to some solid legislation that benefited the country as a whole. At the 2000 Democratic National Convention, however, Al Gore turned in a new direction: the people vs. the powerful. He woke up the hard left that Clinton had effectively sidelined. The electoral defeats of Al Gore and John Kerry buried the center-left. Within months of Kerry's defeat, progressives installed their own favorite, Howard Dean, at the head of the DNC. By the 2008 primaries, Hillary Clinton's occasional mild suggestions that perhaps some progressive rhetoric might come off as a tad extreme outside progressive circles branded her untouchable. When Barack Obama received the nomination, the Clinton machine shifted to serve its new progressive overlords.

By 2015, Hillary's own triangulation landed her squarely between Barack Obama and Bernie Sanders, way off on the progressive far left. During the first primary debate, what remained of the rational, pro-American center-left appeared on stage in the person of Senator Jim Webb. Webb's answers, demeanor, and overall performance were so out of place that nearly all commentators thought that he would have been a better fit for the Republican stage. His candidacy garnered no support. The center-left was dead.

The situation spiraled downhill even faster after the 2016 election. In 2018, the Democrats retook the House of Representatives with a strategically sound slate of candidates. In safe Democrat districts, progressives broke new ground in explicit antisemitism, radical economics, and the mainstreaming of Islamism. In swing suburban districts, Democrats fielded moderate-sounding centrists. Both sets of candidates did well, setting the stage for internal dissension. The moderates never had a chance. The new arrivals positioning themselves for future leadership were young, nonwhite, nonmale, radical progressives.

"The Squad" of Alexandria Ocasio-Cortez, Rashida Tlaib, Ilhan Omar, and Ayanna Pressley topped the list. It took them less than six months to seize control of the caucus. When Speaker Pelosi and other careerist hacks gingerly suggested that perhaps the Squad members might tone down their antisemitic rhetoric, Ocasio-Cortez led the charge in labeling Pelosi a racist. Pelosi recoiled, backed down, and never again challenged them. When Omar and Tlaib faced primary challengers who were equally progressive but less intentionally inflammatory, Pelosi endorsed the Squad members who'd put her in her place.

Radical progressives set the agenda for the 116th Congress. Early on, they elevated ideology over people when they abandoned the "dreamers" they'd claimed to champion as less important than a porous southern border. The absurd coup masquerading as an impeachment attempt that they foisted upon their party—and America—revealed their tenuous relationship with truth, with justice, with equality under the law, and with the American system. Party hacks like Jerry Nadler and Adam Schiff lost whatever shred of credibility they may once have possessed; Schiff in particular took on a glazed look, chairing critical House hearings with the demeanor of a man bewitched. He will go down in history as one of the greatest intentional liars ever to serve in Congress. Or at least he would, if America's press retained even a shred of dignity and responsibility— which means he won't.

By 2020, though more than half the candidates in the Democrats' bloated field of presidential contenders had built careers and reputations as moderates, they competed fiercely for the title of most progressive. If Joe Biden had taken a single stand during his lengthy Senate career that he failed to repudiate in his bid for the nomination, it's because no one had asked him to disown it.

An ideology that had first gelled in opposition to George W. Bush, then flourished beneath the guidance of Barack Obama, finally exploded into a full-blown, delusional, conspiracy-theoretic, insurrectionist hate movement targeting Donald Trump and his supporters. The faculties that had given it life moved beyond propagandizing into full-blown evangelizing. They came to see their sole task as spreading their new creed—rather than, say, educating the students in their charge, or teaching the critical thinking skills allegedly central to a liberal arts education. Social media impelled their efforts into hyperdrive.

These evangelizing ideologues are in firm control of academia, K–12 education, the media, Hollywood, Silicon Valley, and the Deep State. They've seized the once-great—and once proudly American—Democratic Party. They're moving toward dominance of Wall Street, the legal profession, the judiciary, and most professional societies. They define conventional wisdom throughout the social sciences and humanities—and to a lesser but still debilitating extent in the natural sciences. Their long march through the institutions continues. With each passing year, America's glorious founding ideals fade further from significance in each of these fields; where they persist, they've been miscast as oppressive, exploitative, and unjust. The threat to America's future is palpable. The window is closing quickly.

That, in a nutshell, is how the mad ravings once acceptable only in rarefied seminar rooms came to pose a mortal threat to the greatest, freest, noblest nation that humanity has ever devised.

CRITICAL THEORY

The progressive move off campus and into society had been decades in the planning. The Credentialed Elite was finally ready to deploy the Terrified Minorities as a weapon against its true enemy, the American Ambitious.

The attack proceeded on two fronts: social and economic. In 2020, they came together with devastating effect. The economic attack was easy. They'd been laying the groundwork for decades. Progressives pushing homes and college degrees, at hugely inflated prices, onto those unable to afford them had found allies far beyond progressive circles. These policies resulted in vast swathes of the American public drowning in debt—and deeply resentful of the banks that had lent them the money. Following the 2008 financial crisis, government policies far more attuned to rescuing the lenders than the borrowers drove the resentment deeper. The disproportionate representation of minorities among those underwater drove it deeper still.

From there, it was easy enough for progressives to depict capitalism as the problem and socialism as the solution without defining or discussing either term. In 2010, progressives designed Obamacare to centralize authority, increase citizen reliance on government, and create patronage opportunities. It succeeded on all three fronts. In 2020, the Chinese Communist Party released a virus that set the stage for the widespread destruction of small business. Authoritarian progressive governors and mayors across the country put in place shutdown orders designed to shatter local economies, consolidate power, increase reliance on government handouts, and create even further patronage opportunities. So much for the economics.

The social front was even more insidious. It drew upon an area long believed to be part of an American consensus, but that merely proves that even when we think we agree, we don't.

In America today, there are very few proud racists. Almost every American alive in 2020 agrees that racism is evil. Great, right? Not so much. We're talking past each other. What is this "racism" that we all oppose? Most people would define it along the lines of "treating people differently because of their race." That's not a bad intuitive response. Racists have always divided humanity into distinct racial categories, categorized people, and assigned them rules and expectations appropriate to their category. Racists also tend to attribute the behavior of an individual to everyone else they've placed in the same category—and at times advocate punishing an entire category for the behavior of some of its members.

That's racism. It's inexcusable. It's anti-American. It's hardly coincidental that the uneasy compromises with racism built into the Constitution almost tore the country apart. Differentiation by race is fundamentally incompatible with an Americanism under which all are created equal.

That's not, however, what progressives mean when they talk about—or rail against—racism. Progressive Credentialed Elite experts in academia have identified a phenomenon they've chosen to name "structural racism" or "systemic racism" *that is not actually racist*. The progressive Aspen Institute defines structural racism as "a system in which public policies, institutional practices, cultural representations, and other norms work in various, often reinforcing ways to perpetuate racial group inequity." Aspen also explains that "structural racism is not something that a few people or institutions choose to practice. Instead, it has been a feature of the social, economic and political systems in which we all exist."

In other words, unlike *actual* racism, *structural* racism is part of the ether. It's independent of the racist attitudes, utterances, or behavior of any individual, institution, organization, corporation, or government. It's a classic conspiracy theory in which unseen forces impose deep inequities upon society whether or not anyone participates actively.

This newly identified phenomenon is grounded in a plausible reading of history as a series of battles between groups that see themselves as distinct, in which the winner imposes its will on the loser. Progressives then feed that observation through some dreadful academic garbage called "critical theory" (or when applied to race, "critical race theory"), that sees all interactions between people or groups as struggles over power, in which an oppressor always imposes unfair terms on the oppressed. Thus, every existing social structure— down to the family—is inherently unjust.

That's what progressives oppose when they call themselves "anti-racist." They're not fighting actual discrimination, dangerous ste-reotyping, or even harmful attitudes. They're fighting the "systems in which we all exist." That's not what most Americans think we're fighting when we oppose racism. It is, however, a wonderful illus-tration of incremental outrageousness: beginning with the well-grounded observation that conquerors often impose their will on the conquered, academics derived "scientific proof" that existence is racist and the nuclear family is a tool of oppression.

Racism and structural racism are distinct phenomena calling for diametrically opposed correctives. The corrective to racism is a colorblind society. Martin Luther King Jr. was the prophet of anti-actual-racism, following in the footsteps of the great Frederick Doug-lass. His dream of a country in which we're each judged as individu-als, by the content of our character rather than the color of our skin, remains a dream—though America has made remarkable advances toward making it a reality. Anti-actual-racists reject any laws, preferences, or behaviors making America less than colorblind. Traditional Americans, who are overwhelmingly antiracist and colorblind, revere MLK and his message.

The corrective to structural racism is very different. To progressives, our 1964 announcement that we decided to prohibit racism and march toward a colorblind society was nice and all, but it left intact all of the structures and inequities built during our years as a society in which racism was acceptable. The only way to correct structural racism is to preserve those structures of preference while inverting the preferences. Most progressives give lip service to King, but their hearts are with Marcus Garvey, Malcolm X, the Black Panthers, and other black separatists. They want black Americans—and all minorities, really—to live in "safely" segregated spaces, impoverished, terrified, enraged, and mired in victimhood until society at large grants them the compensation they deserve. For structural racism to end, the "white people" whose "privilege" built the status quo must suffer. Only then can justice prevail.

In other words, traditional American opponents of *actual* racism strive for a world with less racism. Progressive opponents of *structural* racism strive for a world with corrective racism. What appears to be a point of agreement is really a point of bitter contention.

It's also a point of extreme confusion. Progressives have weaponized that confusion to devastating effect. They've deployed it to mobilize Terrified Minorities, paralyze corporate America, and cripple the small businesses that power the American Ambitious. Progressive critical theorists fostered the idea that all interactions between people assigned to different races are inherently racist and oppressive.

Beginning at least as early as the death of Trayvon Martin in 2013, the dangerous myth of systemic racism became entrenched. When

George Floyd—a troubled man in the midst of a fentanyl overdose—died in the custody of the Minneapolis police, the public was already primed to accept the charges of racism as a matter of course. No one bothered to ask for evidence that there was a racial motive at play in the incident. Actual racism was irrelevant; all that mattered was that a black man dying in police custody exemplified systemic racism. The carefully choreographed release of a grisly video and the withholding of exculpatory body cam evidence and a tox screen were enough to inflame passions.

Radical organizations preaching actual racism in opposition to systemic racism—many linked to the anti-American, antisemitic, antifamily Black Lives Matter movement (or the Movement for Black Lives)—surged forward to capture the American mainstream. Working in alliance with thuggish Antifa shock troops, they launched an attack on American cities, a protection racket extracting "donations" from American corporations, and an illegal scheme funneling "charity" into the pockets of the Democratic Party. They came away with an impressive haul. It seems likely that many of the donors thought they were supporting something very different from the racist, radical, progressive groups they actually funded.

By the end of 2020, the progressive plan was in full view. The Credentialed Elite was richer and more powerful than ever. Minorities were terrified, enraged, and violent. The American Ambitious were in a chokehold. A rigged election put progressives in charge of the federal government. The progressive system that had graduated and moved beyond campus twenty years earlier had done itself proud.

4

AMERICA'S TRANSFORMERS

NOBLES AND PEASANTS

Let's step back from considering how progressives attack to consider who progressives are and how they live. Ideological progressivism is a movement of the elite, by the elite, for the elite. Committed ideological progressives skew considerably above average on both formal education and income. Progressives spend more years in school and collect more degrees than the average American. It's a mistake, however, to refer to them as "the educated." Today's progressives have been grossly miseducated. The primary goal of progressivism is to keep the Credentialed Elite living comfortably and feeling morally superior to the rest of American society while holding the masses at bay.

After their university indoctrination, progressives head off to live in progressive enclaves, mostly in coastal cities or college towns, where they have few children. Progressives with training in something useful get high-paying jobs in technology, media, finance, law, education, entertainment, or government. Progressivism dominates these critical sectors so completely that those who do not subscribe to its ideological edicts frequently feel the need to hide their true beliefs and feelings.

Young progressives with degrees in ethnic or gender studies, or otherwise lacking useful skills, gravitate toward service industries supporting their more qualified peers, hoping to parlay a stint as a barista or an Uber driver into some role at a start-up launched over their lattes or in their back seats. While waiting, the more ambitious among them seek to leverage their degrees in grievance studies into actionable political grievances capable of generating viral rage. Those lacking both skills and ambition still choose to live in pricey progressive enclaves, playing the important roles of drifters and hangers-on, ensuring the steady supply of parties, drugs, sex, and the sheer number of bodies needed to fill protests and make viral campaigns viral.

It's an interesting sociology, but it's not for everyone. In fact, it can't be for everyone. If everyone tried to play, the economy would collapse. For society to function, somebody, somewhere, has to engage in physical labor, energy production, grunge work, construction, policing, and various other tasks that progressivism places on a low moral plane. Furthermore, someone, somewhere has to have children.

While such distasteful necessities make progressives unhappy, even progressives understand that they are indeed necessary. Progressivism thus accommodates these needs by working to ensure that the "somewhere" is far from their own enclaves, and by disdaining the "someones" as deplorable reactionaries clinging to outdated notions, silly superstitions, and flawed moral codes.

This progressive disdain for nonprogressives poses a clear dilemma: progressives can't get the political power they need for their transformation unless their candidates can secure enough votes—something that progressives alone can rarely deliver honestly. While progressive leaders have politicized key parts of the federal bureaucracy and fought hard against election integrity, their first full-blown rollout in a national election occurred in 2020. Even then, however, it couldn't have worked without the cover story of overwhelming minority support. Progressive leaders understand that they need allies—large voting blocs drawn from the nonprogressives they hold in contempt.

Today's Democratic Party manifests their response: a classic coalition of those living at the top and bottom rungs of society. History is replete with tales of tension between a small group of royals and a large group of nobles, between those nobles and a larger group of merchants, and between those merchants and a still-larger group of peasants. While some societies muddied the distinctions because members of these different economic classes hailed from differing ethnicities or adhered to different faiths, the formulation is robust. We humans are hardwired to demand the perks of the station just above us while fighting to preserve the perks of the station we have already achieved from those clutching at our feet. Contemporary American society is no exception.

The common historical patterns of alliance are equally predictable. The nobility, angling for position vis-à-vis both royalty and merchants, reaches out to the peasants. Peasants make for ideal allies. Peasants tend to live far away from nobles. Peasants interact with merchants on a daily basis, but with nobility only as needed—and then typically at the convenience of the nobles. Peasants are also far happier blaming their problems on a concrete king whose image dominates their existence than on an amorphous noble class.

Most important of all, peasants are cheap. They're easy to scare and easy to bribe—the less educated and poorer they are, the better.

Many a noble has stoked resentment among the peasantry. It's never too hard to spin the tale of a king who sees peasants as useful for little other than working his fields and filling his army—slaves and cannon fodder. The nobles also love to emphasize that greedy merchants seek to squeeze every penny and morsel they can from their customers and tenants, most of whom are peasants. Only the nobility—with whom the peasants have minimal direct contact—actually cares for the peasantry. Only the nobility worries about society at large, with far less ego than the king and far less venality than the merchants. Only the nobility can provide the peasants with the protection they need, and with the assurance that they will go neither hungry nor homeless.

With a good narrative, a few supporting anecdotes, and some table scraps withheld from the king or wrested from the merchants, a savvy nobility can secure the allegiance of a vast, manipulable peasantry. This formidable alliance motivates the king and the merchants to notice that they too share interests. From the king's perspective, a productive merchant class enhances the wealth and reputation of his kingdom, not to mention the tax base. The merchants represent a sizable group of people possessing a clear interest in regime stability. If the king falls—whether to a peasant uprising or to an invading force—the merchants will be easy targets. The king, or perhaps more precisely the king's law, provides the merchants' best guarantee of preserving the benefits of their hard work. Furthermore, the king's constant deliberations about reducing the barriers separating the most successful merchants from the least successful nobles keeps the nobles focused on preserving their own privileges rather than on usurping the privileges of royalty.

This alliance pattern explains the two major political parties in twenty-first-century America. Today's Democrats align America's Credentialed Elite nobility seeking to preserve its own privileged position with the Terrified Minority peasants it has scared and bribed into dependency.

As always, the nobility understands that the health of the alliance hinges upon its ability to keep the peasants afraid, dependent, and distant: afraid of the productive working and business classes of the American Ambitious; dependent upon the crumbs progressive elites manage to "redistribute" from that productive center downward; distant from the very pleasant enclaves of progressive living. That's why progressives spend so much time destroying any member of any minority who strays off the plantation. Informed Minorities would never subject themselves to the horrors the Credentialed Elite inflicts upon them. Only Terrified Minorities embrace such degradation.

Today's progressive Democrats seek to keep the most vulnerable parts of American society poor, ignorant, scared, and dependent. That formula provides the only semi-honest path to progressive political power. Without it, all they've got is outright fraud. As a result, progressives prey relentlessly on America's poorest ethnic communities, on immigrants, and on single women, working overtime to keep them in states of constant fear.

Progressive mythology positions progressivism as a force seeking justice for these vulnerable groups. Nothing could be further from the truth. In fact, progressives seek to bribe them with crumbs and slogans, while working overtime to ensure that they remain terrified, vulnerable, victimized, enraged, and unlikely to seek self-improvement. It's a powerful alliance because progressives are excellent propagandists who dismiss the truth casually while skillfully tugging at heartstrings. Moreover—credit where credit is due—progressives are often the only outsiders willing to approach minorities to pitch their case. No part of the American political spectrum has ever been willing to invest as heavily in cultivating allies within minority communities as the radical left. Coupled with progressive control of American media, entertainment, and academia, the progressive message is often the only one that vulnerable Americans ever hear.

The alliances progressives cultivate are hardly beneficial to the minorities. Progressives promote minority leaders who express rage, victimization, and entitlement with little concern for the welfare of those they claim to represent. Worse, thanks to their media megaphone, progressives spread the racist myth that minority communities speak with a single authentic voice—an enraged anti-American, anti-Western, antitradition voice. Far too many patriotic Americans seem willing to accept those absurd and offensive claims of authenticity. They cower in fear at the thought of being labeled "racist" for opposing progressive racism and questioning the priorities of the abysmal minority leadership progressives have enriched.

Progressivism has weaponized the Terrified Minorities quite effectively. In exchange for progressive platitudes, bribed leaders, and empty promises, progressive elites secure vast minority support. And they do it while depriving those loyal supporters of the family structures, faith institutions, educational opportunities, jobs, training, investments, and neighborhood safety necessary to improve their lives and embrace the American dream. Acting in a manner that would have made any of history's most duplicitous nobilities proud, progressive elites control their minority peasants with table scraps and vitriol, keep them distant from progressive residential enclaves, and trap them in misery and poverty.

Tilting the balance even further to favor the progressive nobility, America's founders not only dispensed with royalty, but ensured that no such class might ever arise. They substituted a Constitution for a king, more elegant in its consistency but far less able to wield autonomous power. As a result, today's Ambitious Americans from the productive merchant middle cling tightly to the Constitution but lack obvious allies. In the absence of a natural royal leader, America's merchant class must stand alone to defend itself from the progressive nobility seeking to hold it back and the peasant masses seeking to tear it down.

The position of America's productive middle would be untenable were it not for American exceptionalism. The American founding embraced ideals that encouraged upward mobility. The unique American combination of individual freedom and personal responsibility, anchored in Judeo-Christian morality and the Anglo-American legal tradition, unleashed human potential like no other system ever devised.

For generations, American children who began life as members of the vulnerable masses—orphans, sharecroppers, captives of company towns, immigrants, and others—found unrivaled opportunity. With each generation, countless peasant children gained the educational and employment opportunities they needed to join America's productive middle and, on occasion, even the elite. Their parents, seeing the opportunities America provided, came to identify more closely with the middle to which they aspired than with the masses to which circumstances had consigned them. They hoped to parlay their own ambitions and hard work to become successful members of the American Ambitious.

The American Ambitious middle, for its part, became one of history's least protective classes. Seeing their own opportunities for mobility—whether ascending through the varied ranks of the middle or breaking through to the elite—productive Americans welcomed newcomers who shared their own work ethic and commitment to productivity. Granted, many members of the American Ambitious resented those who shot past them, but they tempered that resentment with an instinctive understanding of the merits of the American system. The end result is that America's productive middle is uniquely magnanimous, dynamic, and large. It's so large, in fact, that if it holds together, it can defeat the combined might of the progressive elite and its peasant allies.

The elites thus deploy two of their most powerful weapons to forestall such a defeat: complexified regulatory rulemaking and rigged electoral competition. Complex regulations distract producers and drain resources. Rigged elections secure elite control. They're two bodies of law that serve no societal purpose other than reducing the productivity of the American Ambitious and preserving elite authority. They keep America's producers reeling.

Under normal circumstances, it would be the king who held the productive middle together, providing it with a unifying cause and ideology. In the antimonarchical US, the productive middle must find its unifying leadership among an unlikely assortment of business leaders—the most successful of the productive American Ambitious—and the Renegade Credentialed strong enough to bear the censure of their peers.

Business leaders, however, tend to be action oriented. They either provide significant funding to the effort or undertake direct action themselves. They operate from a deep instinctive and experiential understanding, but rarely construct elegant narratives. They behave strategically without detailing comprehensive strategies. They balance ideology and pragmatism, typically exhibiting greater pride in their achievements than in their principles.

Narrative, strategy, coherence, explanation, presentation, and education fall to us renegades. We Renegade Credentialed are demographically indistinguishable from the progressive elites. We've been to the same schools, earned the same degrees, and entered the same professions. We live in progressive enclaves, where our tastes and hobbies align with those of our progressive neighbors, colleagues, friends, and families. We differ from progressives in two critical ways: we tend to feel far more rooted in history and tradition, and we tend to have far thicker skins. Our affinity for history and tradition binds us to the productive middle of the American Ambitious. The thick skins let us function in progressive enclaves.

Fortunately, we renegades do have one thing going for us. We've watched, internalized, and studied progressivism well enough to understand it and to reject it. We know how progressives think, and why their thinking is flawed. Very few of our progressive neighbors can say the same about us. They don't know what makes us tick, why we've rejected progressivism, how we can tolerate standing with the productive middle, or why we think it's important to provide actual help to minorities, women, and the poor. That lack of awareness tends to make them skittish and prickly.

That's a very dangerous position for a group that considers itself to be intellectually superior. At the end of the day, it's that very fear that will bring down the ideological progressive intelligentsia: an intellectual movement terrified by ideas, debates, and discussions can never stand in the long run. It can, however, impose significant damage in the short run. While that's happening, watch for their hangers on to continue enjoying life in the privileged progressive enclaves even we renegades often call home.

SOCIAL PROGRESSIVES

One of the things you learn living in a progressive enclave is that most self-proclaimed progressives have no idea what progressivism is. They're progressive for purely social reasons. Most think progressivism is a synonym for decency. Some suggest that as human understanding and knowledge progresses, our social, cultural, and governmental structures should reshape themselves in light of that progress. That's an eminently reasonable belief and a perfectly plausible use of the word "progressive." It just happens to be wrong when applied to contemporary progressivism.

To compound their error, they contrast that misunderstanding of "progressivism" with "conservatism," which they caricature as a preference for bad ideas that have become comfortable and accepted over ideas that "science can now prove" are superior. Of course, not only has science *not* proved that most of their new ideas are superior, but anyone who thinks that science *could* offer proof one way or the other understands neither science nor proof. Still, it makes them feel good to say such things.

Relatively few of these "social progressives" are even aware that progressivism is an actual, living, evolving ideology. They don't know that progressivism embodies a set of beliefs. They don't know that progressivism preaches a rigid moral code. Forget knowing what those beliefs and morals are—or how they compare to those of other ideological systems—most social progressives are blissfully unaware that such things exist. They describe themselves as progressives because belonging to the decent crowd is good for their social lives, good for their professional advancement, and—above all—good for their self-esteem.

For the most part, social progressives have solid American instincts. They have no idea that their actions, their activism, their donations, and their votes have been working to undermine the American republic. They've been seduced. They're marching blissfully to their own destruction. Worse, they're following it to our destruction.

Once they start rooting for the Blue Donkeys, everything falls into place. They forgive the "good guys" on their team for almost everything and cheer on the lynch mobs attacking the other team's "bad guys" for minor oversights or misstatements. They can't really tell you why they feel so strongly about the game, but they really, really don't appreciate it when anyone notices their inconsistencies and hypocrisies. They feel challenged when pushed for facts or original sources. They get angry when asked to explain why they hold the positions they hold. They resent anyone who puts forward evidence-based arguments that make them feel bad.

Their politics is more instinctive than analytic. They pick their favorite buzzwords, slogans, and litmus test issues; they don't sit around conducting deep policy analyses. They believe what they read in the *New York Times*, see on CNN, and absorb through the mainstream media—though they do concede that whenever the story involves facts they know personally, the coverage is entirely wrong.

In that, social progressives are rather typical Americans. They don't live and breathe politics. They stand out, however, because they consider themselves educated and wrap their egos in being smart. People who wrap their egos elsewhere—in being kind, loving, strong, rich, hard-working, loyal, etc.—often remain open to learning new things, changing their minds, and deciding that their previous beliefs had been wrong. People who wrap their egos in their own superior intelligence have a far harder time doing so. Social progressives living in America's elite coastal enclaves who face the truth about progressivism will have to admit that they've been wrong—while the backward, deplorable, immoral yahoos of flyover country have been right. That's a serious blow to their egos.

Social progressives thus cling tightly to their misguided ideology, often to their own detriment and against their own better judgment. In fact, most of them recognize that progressivism is wrong about whatever subject matter they know best. Progressives on Wall Street readily confess that progressivism is dead wrong about economics and finance. Progressives in law enforcement wish that progressive leaders appreciated the steps they take to keep minority and immigrant neighborhoods safe. Jewish progressives lament the apparent confusion that leads so many progressives to embrace antisemitism. I even have an activist progressive friend (or perhaps ex-friend, given that progressives tend to shun anyone capable of seeing through their nonsense) who committed his career to education reform; he insists that his fellow progressives simply "don't understand" that teachers unions are the problem while school choice is the solution.

All of these social progressives share the firm belief that progressivism (whatever it may be) is an ideology profoundly committed to justice, peace, equality, and a better world. They all share the belief that progressivism is an imperfect ideology, whose most significant error—by sheer coincidence—occurs in the policy arena they themselves best understand. They all bristle at the suggestion that progressivism is no closer to advocating reasonable solutions to the challenges they don't study than it is to those closest to home. So, yes. They are indeed proud progressives. Just don't ask them what that means, or they'll get angry, defensive, and—far too often—abusive. After all, they're not just defending their political preferences. They're defending their egos.

The success of the ideological progressives at selling their lies explains how so many people who pride themselves on their decency, their compassion, their innate sense of justice, and their commitment to making the world a better place might want to consider themselves progressives. Social progressives seek out and support progressive causes, organizations, and politicians—completely unaware of what they're actually supporting. While they think they're reaching out to like-minded, decent people and groups committed to improving the world, they're actually latching on to ideological progressives committed to furthering an ideology that opposes all of those ideals.

Such tragic misconceptions are hardly restricted to the term "progressive." According to quite a few recent polls, many otherwise decent respondents associate the word "socialism" with positive ideals that have little to do with actual socialist ideology or practice. Millions of decent Americans who oppose actual racism, and who believe that all lives possess equal inherent dignity and value, have thrown their support behind blindingly racist, antifamily, antifaith, antisemitic, anti-American organizations operating beneath the "Black Lives Matter" banner. Therein lies the tragedy. Most social progressives end up supporting organizations and candidates whose goals they oppose, while fighting and defaming those whose goals they support.

In short, social progressives have been seduced. They may not know what progressivism is, but they associate it with positive things. Then they support it because, well, who would oppose positive things?

CORE PROGRESSIVISM

So, what is progressivism? "Trust the experts" is a bumper sticker. It's not terribly satisfying. If we really want to understand the phenomenon, we'll have to dig a bit deeper.

First, progressivism derives from the utopian tradition. All utopians believe that humanity is perfectible. The flaws we witness today exist because flawed societies force people to make selfish decisions just to survive. The key to perfecting humanity is perfecting society. A perfect society will present only the incentives for elevated behavior. Thus, all problems exist because of offensive societal structures.

All solutions begin with a restructuring of society. This view stands in stark contrast to the Judeo-Christian tradition, in which only God is perfect, people are inherently flawed, and social structures exist to help people control and channel their negative inclinations in directions that benefit society at large.

Second, progressivism focuses on group injustice rather than on the actions of the individual. In the progressive view of history, identifiable groups declared themselves distinct from, and superior to, "others." They then seized power for themselves, exploited the others, and built social structures to entrench their exploitative privilege. Though some members of each group were always better off than—and behaved differently from—others, those differences paled in comparison to the similarity of their positions as members of the same group within the hierarchy. Progress toward a perfect society requires shattering the structures that preserve privilege while retaining the group distinctions and changing the pecking order of privilege. Once past and future have been brought into balance, society will have progressed to its next, more elevated and enlightened, state. This view stands in sharp contrast to the notions of individual liberty and personal responsibility that underpin America's foundational documents and principles.

Third, progressivism internalizes its own inevitability. The arc of history bends toward justice, and all. Those who fight to preserve a structurally unjust status quo are doomed to fail in the long run, but they may delay the march toward justice. The only true threat to social justice prevailing is cataclysmic—a destruction of the environment so widespread that it wipes out human life. Contrast that view with President Reagan's warning: "Freedom is never more than one generation away from extinction."

Fourth, progressivism recognizes the inherent moral superiority of elite progressives—even better if they're part of the Credentialed Elite. Every movement needs a vanguard, a priesthood, or some other group elevated above all others to push forward with the important work of guiding society. Some movements let the citizens choose their own leaders, but elitist movements typically prefer to play it safe. They elevate their own greatest ideologues to elite status, keep them elite as long as they continue to tout the ideology, and devise intricate schemes to keep down the masses. Progressivism is a classic elitist movement—precisely what you'd expect a movement of the Credentialed Elite to be. This idealized elite represents the polar opposite of Thomas Jefferson's own idealization of the yeoman farmer.

To put the matter concisely, progressivism is a leftist ideology that derives from the utopian tradition, focuses on group injustice rather than on individual action, believes in its own inevitability, and recognizes the inherent superiority of elite progressives. The entire progressive moral code flows from those core beliefs—particularly the notion that "enlightened" elite opinion of the moment defines morality, while all other opinions are immoral. It rejects the Judeo-Christian tradition and numerous core beliefs of the American founding.

Progressivism's own core beliefs translate easily into politics and policy. Nearly every position progressives hold dear is cast as holding back the members of a "historically privileged" group, elevating representative members of a "historically exploited" group, or preventing an environmental cataclysm capable of derailing human progress toward social justice. In actuality, most progressive policies entrench the elite status of ideological progressives; any contribution they make toward their claimed objectives is purely coincidental. Of course, there's no way the leftist academic ideologues who devised this evil and self-serving ideology could have sold it had they tried to do so honestly. They never bothered trying. Seduction is so much more effective.

At the end of the day, ideological progressives adhere to a classic utopian formulation: What drags humanity down is a deeply flawed society. Create the perfect society, and perfect human behavior will follow. The sequence is always the same. First promote elite ideology. Then eliminate the deplorables. Balance and eliminate the inequities of the past. A perfectly just society will emerge. Each member will work hard and produce because society demands it. From each according to his ability, to each according to his need.

It's hard to think of a formula that has been tried and failed more often.

LIES, LIES, LIES

"Who controls the past controls the future; who controls the present controls the past." That was Orwell. Who controls language controls the present. That's me. Maybe some other folks. But since it wasn't Orwell, I can claim credit.

Progressives came to own American education and communication by seizing control of our language. Since taking control, they've twisted countless words to mean their opposites. That's let them claim that good is bad and bad is good. That's deadly. Words are the building blocks of reality. To win—to restore America—we must retake our language. Soon.

Some of the deadliest weapons in the progressive arsenal are linguistic: deconstruction, fabrication, and projection. That's three different ways of saying that progressivism rests upon lies, but they're very specific and very different types of lies.

Progressivism has implemented a brilliant division of labor. Deconstruction is an academic pursuit. Members of the Credentialed Elite change the meaning of words to suit their tastes, then broadcast the new definition as a "scientific advance." Fabrication falls to the progressive media. Their job is to turn invented talking points into conventional wisdom through sheer repetition—and more recently, by suppressing inconvenient facts and uncomfortable opinions. Projection belongs to progressive politicians and activists. Only those fully aware of the plan can accuse the opposition of planning it. Deconstruction, fabrication, projection. When used together, their effect can be devastating.

Deconstruction got its start as a theory of language. The first deconstructionists—Credentialed Elite thinkers of the 1960s New Left—put forward the idea that words have no fixed meaning. Everything depends upon context. Given that the context surrounding a speaker differs from the context surrounding a listener, effective communication can become quite challenging. The situation is even worse with written language; writers and their readers often live in contexts so different that the quest for common meaning seems ludicrous.

Deconstruction flourished among the Credentialed Elite. It was precisely the type of gibberish that thrives in academic environments. It quickly flowered into an academic movement intent upon stripping meaning from life. Facts, truth, and reality all became subjective. Notoriety and celebrity replaced virtue and achievement. Judgmentalism and moralizing replaced judgment and morality. Nothing was known, nothing was settled, nothing was real. Every object, every concept, every relationship came untethered. A new world beckoned. A better world. A world of justice. A progressive world.

Progressivism seized control of language with deconstructionist tools like political correctness, microaggressions, and dog whistles. The words a speaker utters, the intent behind the utterance, the context in which it is uttered, no longer matter. What matters is the most negative way that a listener—often a distant third-party listener spoon fed a shred of text shorn of context—might perceive the utterance. For good measure, progressive pundits are always eager to tell their readers how to read invidious intent—racism, misogyny, or "attacks on democracy"—into any seemingly innocuous statement from anyone they've chosen to attack.

Progressivism weaponized deconstruction. Progressives need never define the words they use, their beliefs, or the standards they propose, because progressive definitions are never fixed. That's particularly true of definitions attached to favored attack terms. To progressives, today's racism need not have anything to do with racism of the past. Stances on LGBTQ rights that were moral yesterday may be immoral today. Sexual overtures that may have been socially acceptable—even welcome—when made decades in the past become harassment and abuse in the rearview mirror.

The most important and successful of all progressive deconstructions involves their favorite—and most overused—word. Racism. Progressives pride themselves, perhaps above all, on being antiracist. The problem is, they aren't. At least, not if you believe that the term "racism" has a fixed meaning. Because if you applied the longstanding, conventional, proper definition of the term, it would become immediately obvious that progressivism is racist at its very core. There's no way that the leading ideological, intellectual, and academic progressives could let that message get out. It would destroy their ability to seduce social progressives and terrify minorities.

So instead, they deconstructed the term. Rather than fighting actual racism, progressives struggle against "structural" or "systemic" racism—phenomena that are not, in fact, racist. To the contrary, nearly all progressive correctives to structural racism are examples of actual racism.

The numerous scenes of racial division, degradation, submission, and penance from the 2020 regime-change protests were particularly graphic, but they were only incrementally outrageous. Videos of "white people" bowing before (or washing the feet of) "black people" at "antiracist" demonstrations? Nothing to see here. After all, "antiracist" progressives had already proudly exempted "women of color" from standard notions of decency. No less a luminary than Democratic Whip Jim Clyburn—the kingmaker whose endorsement on the eve of the South Carolina primary effectively handed Joe Biden the Presidency—applied that exemption to excuse the shockingly overt antisemitism, anti-Americanism, slander, fabrication, Holocaust denial, and hatemongering the Squad brought to Congress in 2019. The progressive promotion of actual racism as a corrective to structural racism wraps deconstruction and incremental outrageousness in a neat little package.

Confused? If not, you're not paying attention. Because progressives control culture, they get to deconstruct and redefine words. If you're a social progressive, you can be forgiven for failing to keep up with every change because your intentions are pure. If you're a more traditional American, you have no leg to stand on: you're a transgressor with ill intent. In fact, you're deplorable.

Weaponized deconstruction handed progressives control of the language. They leveraged that control to deconstruct reality with their second great weapon, fabrication. To state the matter simply, progressives lie. Constantly. About everything. They don't even care if their story is plausible. Because progressives dominate print, broadcast, and social media, they turn whatever story they want to tell into conventional wisdom. Every committed progressive understands that a lie told often enough becomes the truth, so they repeat their lies. Often. Then they report on the previous day's reported lies, repeatedly raising concerns that if true, would be serious. Of course, they're not true—but if they were, wouldn't the public have a right to know? And when many people relate variants of the same potentially concerning story, isn't that alone cause for concern?

Fabrication works because the progressive media bombards America with fake news, knowing that enough of it will take root to inflict the desired harm. Progressive fabrication reached stratospheric proportions with a conspiracy theory called "Russia Collusion." That deeply delusional and implausible tale rested upon zero hard evidence, zero circumstantial evidence, and a handful of reports that never passed the smell test. But to progressives, it was gospel. Astoundingly, even when their web of innuendo, inference, and flights of fancy imploded, it remained progressive gospel. Many subsequent progressive fabrications—including their coup attempt masquerading as an impeachment—built upon it. It's thus worth recalling what it was that progressives believed from day one of this fabrication. The tale went something like this:

Russia's authoritarian leader, Vladimir Putin, had done well for his country with Obama in the White House. He'd reestablished Russian power in the Middle East, annexed Crimea, destabilized eastern Ukraine, taken possession of much of North America's uranium, built up his military capabilities, deepened his ties to Iran and Turkey, and positioned himself to dominate Europe's energy supply.

Surveying the American political terrain, he saw that Hillary Clinton, who'd helped create the openings Russia had exploited, was favored to become the next president. Over the years, Putin's cronies had channeled loads of money through the Clinton Global Initiative. He could guess that as president, Hillary would bring back her State Department team that had proved so accommodating. He also knew that Democrats had a history of towing soft lines on both Russia and US defense, and that no matter how soft a line Hillary chose, elements of her own party would push her to be even softer. Putin, like everyone else, would have expected her to build upon the Obama legacy in Iran and Syria that had already proved so favorable to Russia. He would have doubted that Clinton would block any of the deals he'd cut with her Davos pals running Germany and the EU.

Panicking for no conceivable reason at the thought of the Obama's policies continuing under Clinton, Putin decided to activate a political novice with a background in real estate and entertainment he'd been cultivating since his days in the old Soviet KGB. He pushed his puppet through the Republican Party to ensure that the American factions most antagonistic toward Russia gained seats in the new administration. Deploying an understanding of the American electorate so savvy that it put every American political professional to shame, Putin sent a few hundred thousand dollars to Eastern European hackers to wage an election-altering social media campaign. Meanwhile, the Trump campaign engaged in a clumsy pattern of dispatching low-level volunteers with zero relevant training to meet Russian spies—just to call attention to the relationship.

It all worked brilliantly. Putin orchestrated a conspiracy running counter to Russia's national interests to pull an electoral upset so stunning that a majority of America's political and media professionals still can't believe it happened.

Because, you know, misogyny.

Right.

"Russia Collusion" is a classic progressive fabrication. It makes no sense, and there's no evidence to support it. But millions believe it, leading congressional progressives will go to their graves swearing it's true, it's inflicted real pain on its targeted victims, and it's harmed the country. Like all conspiracy theories, the total absence of both motive and evidence only proves its truth.

Want a more plausible story that actually fits the facts? Putin knows that the greater any country's internal problems, the lesser its ability to project power abroad. Surveying the American terrain, he concluded that political polarization was the most likely source of internal tension in the US. He invested in a run-of-the-mill propaganda operation to stoke that polarization. He spent most of his time bashing the favorite because stoking resentment against the next president makes far more sense than turning the winners against a quixotic losing candidate.

Putin got that last part wrong—just like most of the planet. The favorite lost. But, boy, did Putin reap a return on his investment! Polarization shot through the roof. A progressive "resistance" movement arose to hamstring the new president's ability to govern—with a particular constraint placed on his freedom of movement vis-à-vis Russia. Putin spent pocket change on a losing ticket and still won the lottery.

While there were indeed a few brave, isolated souls reporting a "Russia story" that made sense, the progressive fabrication drowned them out. By sheer repetition, the progressive fable became enshrined as conventional wisdom.

All of which leads to the next question: Why this particular fable? The answers are rooted in the third great progressive weapon: projection. Ideological progressives have long had plans to protect their dominance. As soon as the Tea Party was born as a potential threat in 2010, the progressive media and the progressive Deep State conspired to strangle it in its cradle. The Obama administration weaponized the Internal Revenue Service to throttle and terrorize grassroots organizations advocating small government, lower taxes, free-market alternatives to Obamacare, prolife activism, the freedom of religion, or support for Israel. Those efforts may well have tipped the balance in the 2012 election.

Empowered, the progressive juggernaut rolled on. During Obama's second term (if not earlier), the political weaponization extended to the FBI, the CIA, the Department of Education, and the Civil Rights Division of the Department of Justice—to name the most obviously compromised agencies. Progressives challenged every measure intended to promote voter integrity, bizarrely insisting that only racists oppose voter fraud. Attorneys General Holder and Lynch backed a mythology of institutional racism plaguing police departments across the country and supported the Marxist racial agitators who arose to promote it. The Department of Education warned that universities preserving due process for students risked losing substantial federal funding.

It was the intelligence community, however, that suffered the greatest politicization. Hillary Clinton's campaign employed foreign intelligence sources to fabricate tales about her opponent. With the Deep State, state-by-state election operatives, and the Clinton campaign all working to ensure that the United States would never again experience a free and fair election, all that remained was projection: Progressive leadership had turned America's premiere intelligence and enforcement agencies into political weapons? Accuse Trump of authoritarianism. Progressive election officials and judges corrupted the voter rolls? Accuse Republicans of trying to rig the elections. Clinton, Obama, Biden, and other leading Democrats had been selling influence to foreign powers for decades? Accuse Trump of selling influence to foreign powers. Progressives planned to riot and resist if Trump won? Accuse Trump supporters of planning to riot and resist if Trump lost.

It was all there in the open. It's always in the open. Projection signals America as to what progressives are planning. Every accusation progressives hurl against their opponents reveals a progressive plan to seize or retain control. Facts? Evidence? Meh. Those sorts of things are purely optional in progressive circles. Nice when you have them, but hardly critical. Why master fabrication if you're going to get hung up on evidence? In progressive morality, the ends justify the means. Deconstructing words, fabricating stories, and projecting ill intent are all morally compelled. Progressives lie constantly, brazenly, and proudly to further their cause.

All of which leads to a question so obvious that Hillary Clinton wrote a whole book fabricating answers: What happened? In the real world, the answer is clear. Progressives got overconfident. America got lucky—or blessed. Luck and blessings are wonderful things, but they're not enough. Progressives had no intention of making the same mistake twice. The 2020 election showed that they learned their lesson well.

FAKE NEWS

Let's talk some more about fabrication, or as it's become known, fake news. Academia may be where progressive thinkers hatch their vile theories, but most of America doesn't flock to seminar rooms for kicks. No, to bring those theories into our living rooms, the Credentialed Elite require the assistance of their loyal students. Mainstream American media, from top to bottom, is a progressive enterprise. The very best mainstream outlets, like the *Wall Street Journal*, try to balance their progressive leanings with other views. Most, following the lead of the *New York Times*, stopped pretending long ago.

America's leading mainstream media outlets are central to progressivism. Their critical job is to turn progressive lies into conventional wisdom. Over time, the progressive media has developed a series of techniques for steamrolling progressive lies into accepted truths. In an attempt to preserve what little is left of their credibility, however, progressive media outlets try to remain cautious. They move forward one step at a time—and they test each new technique in a narrow, isolated setting before rolling it out fully. It's the academic incentive system in play. Incremental outrageousness is the order of the day in America's newsrooms.

Traditionally (i.e., prior to the Trump presidency), the progressive testbed of choice has been Israel. If you want to see how progressivism will attack America next year, study its fabricated attacks on Israel last year. In September 2000, when Yasir Arafat unequivocally rejected a peace offer granting him everything to which the leftist "international community" claimed he was entitled, fake news blamed Israel. When Arafat's rejection included his roll-out of a long-planned terror war, fake news blamed an Israeli politician (then out of power), Ariel Sharon, for triggering the war with a "provocative" visit to Judaism's holiest site. Public outcry against the media fabrication was muted. The technique had proven itself. Fake news reporting of the Bush administration's campaign to free Iraq from Saddam's totalitarianism followed an eerily similar path.

Perhaps even more ominous, the opening salvos of Arafat's terror war included a prominent hoax perpetrated by French media: film footage allegedly showing an Arab boy named Muhammad al-Durrah killed in a crossfire. Though subsequent investigations showed that the entire event had been staged, the scene inflamed passions throughout the Islamic world. Fast forward twenty years to the passions surrounding the video of George Floyd, and the parallels become terrifying.

With the rise of Barack Obama, fake news came into its own.

From top to bottom, the Obama administration's propagandists encouraged and abetted it. The Obama team helped the fabrications branch beyond foreign policy—where the broad public's lack of personal exposure to the facts made them easy to sell—into the domestic arena, where many in the media had long assumed that people would believe their own experiences rather than the preferred progressive lies.

Fake news was instrumental in selling the Obamacare debacle to a skeptical nation; Jonathan Gruber, one of its key architects, later laughed at the gullibility of an American public willing to believe their president's intentional lies. Fake news helped Ambassador Susan Rice convince the American public that Libyan Arabs in Benghazi were mindless savages, easily pushed into deadly rage upon learning of an obscure YouTube video—rather than strategic, methodical anti-American terrorists. Fake news promulgated the mythical epidemic of racist cops oppressing black communities throughout the country, promoting riots and reversing decades of advances in the fight against racism. The Obama team fully endorsed the crown jewel of America's fake news: the bizarre notion that the eschatological tale of climate change has something to do with science, and that the opinion of "97 percent of scientists" somehow justifies authoritarianism.

Obama's signature foreign policy item, his abysmal Iran deal, would have been dead on arrival had it not been for fake news. Ben Rhodes, Obama's deputy national security advisor for strategic communications, later boasted of his adroit exploitation of a gullible, unethical media to create a useful echo chamber. A deal whose clear objective was strengthening Iran—enriching its treasury, improving its economy, empowering its military, expanding its irregular terrorist forces, entrenching its virulently anti-American theocracy, curtailing its liberal dissidents, and legitimizing its nuclear program—was sold to the American public as a means of restraining Iran.

Fake news was a central part of Obama's governing strategy. Without fake news, he never could have sold the American public on Obamacare, Benghazi, structural racism, climate change, the Iran Deal, and numerous other debacles of foreign, domestic, and economic policy.

By the time Donald Trump announced his candidacy in June 2015, America's fake news media had refined their methods. Rolling them out fully was easy, less expensive than actual reporting, and good for ratings—at least until Trump began to call them out for what they are: enemies of truth and enemies of the American people. Hit for the first time with a leader eager to tell the American public what its press had become, the country's finest purveyors of fake news wrapped themselves in the First Amendment. They insisted loudly that the suggestion that a responsible press would maintain at least a pretense of journalistic ethics was an infringement upon press freedom. That too was a fabrication.

In fact, the *New York Times* ran a rare front-page editorial in August 2016 explaining why it was abandoning even the pretense of journalistic integrity in favor of ensuring that Donald Trump did not win the election. Not to be outdone, the *Huffington Post* appended a disclaimer to every article mentioning the GOP's candidate: "Editor's note: Donald Trump regularly incites political violence and is a serial liar, rampant xenophobe, racist, misogynist, and birther who has repeatedly pledged to ban all Muslims—1.6 billion members of an entire religion—from entering the U.S." Overall, it was an impressive string of defamatory lies. It was also a brilliant illustration of incremental outrageousness in action. Success in today's progressive media flows to those who have best mastered the incentive system that destroyed academia.

It wasn't the first time the mainstream media confessed its sins to the yawns of America. In 2003, shortly after American troops deposed Saddam Hussein, CNN's chief news executive, Eason Jordan, wrote a *New York Times* column admitting that his network had been lying to make Saddam look good for over a decade; telling the truth would have endangered his reporters. The disclosure had no perceptible effect on CNN's reputation.

Mainstream American media is no longer a credible source of information. Yet anyone who points out the horrible track record of these fabulists-posing-as-reporters gets accused of attacking the First Amendment. America's fake news is as defensive and self-important as it is irresponsible. It's a credit to the Credentialed Elite that trained it.

America's progressive media has also become predictable. Some progressive somewhere fabricates an incredible, obscene tale out of whole cloth. A progressive politician expresses grave concern because, if this unbelievable tale were true, it would indeed be a matter of grave concern. Progressive members of Congress call for investigations, inquiries, subpoenas, and hearings to determine whether or not it's true. The progressive press covers the Congressional hysteria widely and loudly. Eventually, the entire story implodes, as it becomes clear that it was little more than the ravings of some twisted progressive lunatic. Neither the progressives in Congress nor the purveyors of fake news concede that they'd been played for fools. Instead, they leave the American public with a lingering memory and implanted doubts. President Trump calls them out on it, reveals the depth of their depraved game, and correctly labels them purveyors of fake news. It's no wonder the progressive press hates him.

This progressive strategy broke new ground during the 2018 confirmation hearings of Brett Kavanaugh to the Supreme Court. Progressives decided to defame Kavanaugh, an upstanding and moral man who'd spent decades in the public eye, as an alleged gang rapist.

The credibility or motive of the accusers was irrelevant. People— malicious progressive lunatics—alleged that Judge Kavanaugh was a gang rapist. The allegations must have been serious because every Democrat on the Senate Judiciary Committee took them seriously. An ethical reporter would have covered the story as evidence of gullibility, venality, brutality, and dishonesty among progressives, but unquestioning fake news legitimized the defamation. Though it was absurd to believe that Kavanaugh might have been a gang rapist, there was nothing remotely absurd about reporting that he was an *alleged* gang rapist. Because, indeed, he was.

By the time the Democrats got around to concocting their (first) impeachment farce—a very thinly veiled coup attempt—pretty much any defamatory gibberish progressives sought to invent had become fodder for the fake news. When it came to misstating almost everything President Trump said or did about the pandemic, the task was child's play. No one even batted an eyelash when the fake news reported that a wave of violent, destructive, anarchic race riots was "mostly peaceful." Fake news outlets wouldn't have known how to report accurately if they'd want to do so; they'd simply allowed their honesty and integrity muscles to atrophy.

Silly as it may seem, however, fake news is not a joke. It implants rumors in the record of our time and creates lingering doubts among the many passive consumers of news stories. It also reveals a great deal about progressive strategy; it's where progressives reveal their plans through projection. As a totalitarian movement that believes in unleashing economic ruin and violence against those deemed guilty of thought or speech crimes, progressives cannot believe that their adversaries are not equally totalitarian.

The entire coverage of the Trump presidency was an exercise in projection. The progressive media turned Donald Trump—a man who'd spent decades in the public eye without standing out for racism, sexism, misogyny, homophobia, or any of the other litany of horrors suddenly attributed to him—into a fierce Hitlerian monster. Then it forgot that the monster was fictional and cowered in fear at its approach. Progressives did it all while practicing racism, sexism, misogyny, homophobia, antisemitism, defamation, and personal destruction. If progressives really want to be afraid of something horrifying, they need only look in the mirror.

To make matters worse, progressives favor censoring voices they cannot control—including those offering actual news. Academia and, increasingly, social media have chosen to slander all antiprogressive ideas as hateful, then moved to eliminate hate speech. In a maneuver hardly uncommon among monopolists, the progressives controlling America's mainstream media seek to eliminate all messages that compete with their own propaganda. In the finest American tradition, President Trump called the progressive propagandists out for what they are while making no attempt to censor them. The minute the tech giants became convinced that he was no longer positioned to take them to task, their oppressive oligarchic tendencies broke through. Before Trump even left office, Twitter, Facebook, Google, and Amazon had moved to better align America's Internet with the Chinese model. Inspired by China's Communist leaders, these American tech leaders simply decided what constituted acceptable speech and began systematically deplatforming those they saw as threats to the fabricated progressive narrative.

It's hard to underestimate the damage that progressive propaganda, or fake news, is causing. America desperately needs a free press—and it has one. But even more than a free press, America needs a responsible press—something that is painfully far from existing. A trustworthy media is one more American institution in dire need of a restoration.

SCIENCE AND FAITH

The deconstruction and redefinition of racism may be the single most useful progressive weapon, but another deconstructed term comes a close second: science. Since the very dawn of the pandemic, it's been common to hear progressives proclaim reverentially that they "follow the science." But that's hardly where it started. The progressive insistence that their eagerness to follow the recommendation of selected progressive Credentialed Elite scientists who tell them what they want to hear somehow equates to following science they don't understand has been around for decades—far longer than progressivism itself.

Unsurprisingly—at least given what we already know about progressivism—that elevation of science to the almighty arbiter of all things good and necessary would have been impossible were it not for deconstruction. In the real world—that is, the world in which words convey a fixed, accepted meaning—science refers to a method of experimentation, data collection, and inference to better understand the world. Engineers or applied scientists then deploy that knowledge to build useful products. Science can thus be descriptive or constructive. It can't incorporate moral judgments to tell us what we should do when facing difficult choices.

That's what I thought science meant back when I first joined the cult of expertise. Wrong! If I'd been a bit savvier, I'd have understood the difference between the interests of scientific inquiry and the interests of the scientific establishment. If I'd been savvier, I'd have understood that when that establishment attempts to shut down a line of inquiry prematurely, it's because there's money and prestige on the line. Push your research in one direction, you puff up the establishment. Push it in the opposite direction, you could hurt the egos and the pocketbooks of some very big players. If I'd been savvier, I'd have understood that I was stepping on some very sensitive toes. Any time scientists tell you that an obvious line of inquiry is "not worth pursuing," they're telling you that pursuing it will make them look bad because your results will far surpass (and often disprove) their own. Hydroxychloroquine, anyone?

I began my career decidedly lacking in such savvy. I believed that scientific inquiry was inherently open and skeptical. For science to "close" a line of investigation, all relevant questions must have answers. When scientific models can explain everything that has ever happened (with perfect precision) and predict (with perfect accuracy) everything that is about to happen, all questions have answers. In the late nineteenth century, many scientists were getting ready to "close" physics. There were only a few minor questions remaining unexplained. Oops! Those minor points blew up every model of nineteenth century physics—literally.

I became savvier the hard way. My exile from the Credentialed Elite taught me to spot charlatans claiming to act in the name of science. That knowledge helped me disentangle the strands of the story progressives most like to peddle as "settled science" unworthy of skepticism—or, as they often term it, "denial."

While progressives may remain uncertain about certain contours of their belief system, their vision of the end of days is clear. In classic eschatological form, "climate change" warns humanity that a failure to repent and change its ways will result in the earth, seas, and skies rising to smite them down. Progressives love to wrap climate science, resource politics, and their apocalyptic vision into a single story, but these strands are easily disentangled.

The science of climate is straightforward and noncontroversial.

The Earth's climate has never been constant. History records cooler phases and warmer phases, each bringing different costs and benefits distributed unevenly around the globe. Past epochs of warming and cooling have moved fertile land from one area to another, raised and lowered sea levels, and altered the navigability of rivers. The causes of these changes are complex, but it appears likely that surface activity is among them. Until recently, the climactic contributions of surface activity were negligible. In recent centuries, the human population has exploded, as has its ability to harness energy. Surface activity capable of contributing to climate change has grown appreciably.

Scientists have built many models in their attempts to understand climate. Two observations characterize all such models: they exhibit tremendous sensitivity to minor input variations, and few if any of their predictions have been accurate (the few that have been broadly or directionally accurate have failed to predict specifics). Such models are characteristic of weakly understood scientific phenomena.

As I learned the hard way, there's a world of difference between the truths of science and the interests of the scientific community. Scientific communities face many incentives unrelated to improving the world's understanding of science. Institutional funding and individual prestige are at least as important. Those imperatives promote only climate scientists whose models help validate the progressive claim of massive, imminent, cataclysmic climate change; they destroy career opportunities for those presenting skeptical, nuanced, or opposing views.

Under such circumstances, the leading scientific voices on climate lack credibility—much like the highly credentialed twentieth-century scientists working for tobacco companies whose work found no link between smoking and cancer. While that lack of credibility doesn't disprove the progressive apocalypse, it does suggest that the true state of scientific knowledge about the climate is very different from the story that progressive scientists would like to tell. In fact, the state of climate science establishes that models with minimal predictive ability, funded to predict a looming cataclysm and exhibiting severe sensitivity to input specifications, can predict a cataclysmic outcome when given appropriate inputs. Nothing more.

So much for the science. The politics of climate harken back to a debate that has raged at least since Thomas Malthus introduced the notion of resource depletion in the early industrial age. Malthus was deeply concerned that the accelerating use of resources was straining the Earth. He predicted that the world would soon run out of resources. His prescription was that his contemporaries curb their seemingly insatiable appetites, cease experimenting and advancing, and conserve the world's resources. As I learned from Saul and the Club of Rome, concerns about resource depletion have never left the environmental discussion, even as consumption has skyrocketed with no signs of imminent depletion.

The beauty of resource depletion is that it justifies draconian reforms. Surely, no one could think that personal short-term comfort is more important than the future of life on Earth! For those seeking to transform society, the fear of such a cataclysm justifies enforcing massive, widespread behavioral change. More importantly, it justifies centralizing the authority necessary to impose such behavior change on an unwilling population. Climate politics thus follows a venerable and predictable pattern that is completely untethered to climate science; it is, quite simply, political.

Progressive eschatology combines suspect science and authoritarian politics into a dark vision: humanity is living out of harmony with nature. As people revel in their orgiastic consumption of energy, Mother Earth—Gaia—weeps. Her resources, her children, the very elements that make Gaia Gaia are disappearing. Callous, thoughtless mankind bleeds her dry, sapping her essence to fulfill its insatiable, base desires. Gaia screams in pain. The rage builds within her. Benevolent goddess that she is, Gaia has sent a warning. She is warming herself slowly, begging humanity to repent. "Change your ways!" she implores. "Cease your exploitation. If you must consume energy, draw it from resources I can renew. Turn back from your crimes against me, your crimes against your planet, your crimes against nature! For if you do not, the Earth will tremble, the skies will cloud, and the seas will rise to smite you!"

Religion? Cult? Certainly not science. Progressives reject everything that came before them, deconstruct reality itself, and rail against the hateful ignorance of those who prefer to embrace the hard-learned lessons of history. The progressive assault on statues is symptomatic of a new faith working to debase whatever the old-time religions revered. The notion that the emerging true faith must destroy the idols of its predecessors is hardly new; it's central to the stories of both Abraham and Mohammed. The summer of 2020 had many hallmarks of a religious awakening. It may mark the moment that progressivism becomes Progressivism—with a capital P—no longer a mere cult of expertise, but soon to become the established religion of the postrepublican United States.

The birth of a new faith is always a dangerous time. Immature faiths tend toward underconfidence, jealousy, and totalitarian approaches toward heretics and deniers. Their leaders argue bitterly about arcane ideological nuances that seem incomprehensible (and often indistinguishable) to outsiders as they battle their way toward a canonical creed. That's precisely what we're experiencing with contemporary progressivism.

Be afraid. Be very afraid.

5

AMERICAN RESTORATION

STOP TRUSTING THE EXPERTS

Within the progressive culture of the twenty-first century, those of us who stand for traditional American values are fighting a rear-guard action. We're not "conservatives." Only a fool would set out to conserve traditions and institutions America has already lost. Our fight today is counterrevolutionary. We must learn how to fight as restorationists.

Let's take it from the top. Stop trusting the experts! They're in it for themselves, not for us—and certainly not for society at large. Now, let's be clear. There's a vast difference between trusting an expert and recognizing their expertise. For the most part, their training is far narrower than the trust they claim. If you have a question about medicine or epidemiology or the climate, there's no better place to turn than a doctor, an epidemiologist, or a climatologist, respectively.

When they tell you that they've got a model you couldn't understand that gives them an answer curiously consistent with their own interests and largely against your own, however, take it with a grain of salt. They've probably strayed beyond their expertise.

Today's experts like to claim that their understanding of some question that should inform policy or action empowers them to dictate that policy or action. That's where you need to stop trusting them. After all, if you wanted to understand the economic, social, and human costs of shutting down the economy, you'd never approach an epidemiologist. If you wanted to understand what it would take to retrofit every structure in America with energy-efficient technology, you'd never approach a climatologist. Yet it was public health officials who shut down the American economy in response to the viral pandemic of 2020. The Green New Deal calls for retrofitting every building in America because an alleged "97 percent of climate scientists" agree about aspects of climate change.

That's nuts! Yet we do it time after time after time. Should we value experts who can help inform our decisions? Absolutely. Should we let them impose decisions upon us because of their greater credentialing? Not a chance.

Worse, because America's experts all belong to the Credentialed Elite, they've internalized its ethos. As I learned back in my AI days, experts will never admit they've been barking up the wrong tree even when events prove that the advice they've been dispensing has been spectacularly, breathtakingly, dangerously backward.

Perhaps the best recent demonstration of the bankruptcy of experts came in an unlikely and unexpected place: Middle East peacemaking. The Abraham Accords—Israel's genuine, warm peace treaties with a growing number of Arab states—weren't supposed to happen. Obama's secretary of state, John Kerry, gave a series of calm, deliberate, informed speeches explaining why such cooperative treaties were impossible prior to the birth of an independent State of Palestine. Nearly every credentialed expert, Democrat and Republican, agreed with him.

When the Trump administration proved that expert assessment wrong, the experts immediately flew into defensive mode—explaining why, despite all appearances, they'd actually been right. To hear them tell it, fundamental changes in the Middle East, entirely unforeseeable as recently as 2017 and unrelated to President Trump, swept a new dynamic across the region. The best that could be said for Trump is that even his bumbling, belligerent, incoherent foreign policy couldn't derail these positive trends. It's the sort of message the Credentialed Elite typically broadcasts when its long-held orthodoxies become laughable.

Here's a better explanation: the "impossible" happened because the Trump team understood that the post–Cold War expert consensus on the Middle East had produced consistent, spectacular, and varied failure.

Credentialed Elite experts helped George H. W. Bush leave Saddam in power, allow genocidal massacres against Kurds and Shiites, tie up a half-million US troops with no clear mission, and set in place an interminable stalemate.

Credentialed Elite experts helped Bill Clinton resuscitate the moribund PLO to enact its "Phased Plan" for Israel's destruction and launch a terror war—while ignoring the rise of al-Qaida and Islamist terrorism.

Credentialed Elite experts helped George W. Bush shift his focus from Afghanistan to Iraq prematurely, then topple a dictator without a plan for dealing with the bloody, anarchic aftermath.

Credentialed Elite experts helped Barack Obama downplay

Islamist terrorism; reject Israel, the Gulf Arabs, and Egypt, in favor of Iran, the Muslim Brotherhood, and the PLO; and endorse the UN's antisemitic criminalization of Jewish existence in the historic Jewish heartland.

So, when Donald Trump chose to sideline the Credentialed Elite experts, reinvigorate America's ties to the Gulf Arabs, steel the resolve of Muslim leaders fighting Islamism, move the US embassy to Jerusalem, and recognize Israel's annexation of the Golan Heights, he had nowhere to go but up. The worst that could have emerged was a fifth consecutive failed American approach to the Middle East. Instead, Trump produced—by far—America's single most successful approach to the modern Middle East.

How? By sidelining the Credentialed Elite experts, paying attention to facts, and applying common sense.

The stunning success of this approach teaches numerous critical lessons that transcend the specifics of Middle East politics—and that must inform restorationist strategy.

First, it turns out that it was neither Arabs nor Israelis who long rendered Middle East peace impossible. It was Western experts. Blind obedience to the Credentialed Elite can inflict significant harm, consume massive resources chasing utopian unicorns, and produce suffering and death on a massive scale.

Second, the Abraham Accords point to an excellent test for determining when it's best to ignore the experts—even (or perhaps especially) if they're reached a fairly broad consensus. When long-standing, widespread, conventional wisdom about a high-profile issue generates only failure, there's something deeply flawed with that "wisdom." Invariably that flaw is buried deep within the fundamental assumption that all "experts" internalized early in their training and never reconsidered.

The message to restorationists is clear: there are limits to where you can trust the experts. Where expertise generates excellence, it deserves to be lauded. Where expertise produces repeated failure, it deserves to be sidelined. Trust experts to address narrow questions for which they have specialized training and expertise—and in which they have developed a credible track record. Stop trusting experts who believe that their narrow, specialized training gives them great insight into the human condition and social structuring—or who insist that orthodoxies with a dismal track record are nevertheless correct. There may be no better definition of a society's "elite" than those able to remain influential despite consistent and repeated failure. Strategic restorationists will learn from President Trump: sideline experts whose only strategy involves doubling down on a losing hand.

Third, the Abraham Accords teach a critical direct lesson about conflict: most conflicts reach resolution when one side wins and the other loses. The Arab/Israeli conflict has always pitted an imperial Arab claim over the entire Middle East against the legitimacy of Jewish self-determination in the Jewish homeland. Those claims are irreconcilable. Peace became possible only when Arab states started thinking of themselves as independent states who had no claims over Israeli territory—in other words, when the Israeli view prevailed. An American restoration will be sustainable only when the progressive worldview and moral code have receded from popularity and cultural dominance.

Progressives understand that if they don't win decisively, they'll lose. That's why they've adopted scorched-earth tactics. Restorationists must be equally committed to victory—and we must find ways to achieve it without scorching the earth. We'll need to wage a powerful strategic offense and accumulate a collection of savvy defensive strategies. A fourth message the Abraham Accords teach is the importance of playing offense. Some of the easiest victories are likely to arise where progressives have been blinded by their own arrogant lies.

The best place to press an offensive is an arena in which we've granted progressives a monopoly: minority communities. The radical left has seduced and manipulated America's urban minorities for nearly 150 years. Progressives forward hateful, rage-filled, anti-American, minority leaders with little concern for community welfare as the sole authentic voices of their community. Far too many Americans accept that authenticity. Far too many Americans cower in fear of being labeled racist for opposing those leaders.

That's a source of deep shame to the patriotic Americans who must now restore the America they failed to conserve. It's also an opportunity. Like all monopolists, progressives have gotten sloppy. They take the subservience of minority communities for granted. With each passing year, progressives grab more for the Credentialed Elite and offer less to the Terrified Minorities. The progressive alliance now rests far more on fear than on bribery.

The past few years have showed glimmers of an awakening. Elements of America's minority communities are learning to see through the progressive lies. They're beginning to stand for themselves and their communities. They're beginning to #WalkAway. They're ready for new leaders and new alliances committed to communal welfare and American ideals. They're ready to become a full and equal part of a restored America.

A genuine agenda for black lives, for example, would bear no relation to the demands of those rioting in the streets. Rather than feeding rage, victimization, and entitlement, it would address the problems plaguing America's black communities, providing safe streets, stable families, school choice, investment, and jobs. Black churches are likely the key players in such a movement. Faith, community, spirit, and dignity are critical to its emergence. Pastors with vision and clarity need our support. Restorationism must help them reclaim authenticity for community leaders who value welfare over rage.

Progressives may think they own the term "racial justice," but that's only because they've deconstructed both words. Progressivism is an inherently racist ideology with little of value to offer those still suffering from the lingering effects of past and vestigial American racism. President Obama's election, and the extent to which his mainstream critics focused on his abysmal policies rather than on his ethnic identity, proved that patriotic Americans had stopped caring about racial distinctions. That's precisely why progressives ratcheted up their agitation, declared a race war, and terrorized minority communities. Progressivism cannot sustain itself if America's minorities correctly identify progressivism as their oppressor and American ideals as the source of their salvation.

Those seeking real racial justice will see through the progressive lies. They will embrace restorationism if we restorationists reach out to them. True racial justice is an arena in which a strong restorationist offense can claim territory progressives take for granted.

That message extends far beyond America's black community. Some of the most astute students of contemporary Islam have reduced that community's challenge to a simple formula: "Radical Islam is the problem. Moderate Islam is the solution." Progressives uniformly ally themselves with radicals to promote the message that authenticity requires rage, separatism, and compensation. Restorationists must counter with the message that authenticity requires moderation, integration, and welfare. No stronger strategic offense is possible.

A similar formulation can guide a restorationist approach to American workers: Green public sector unions are the problem. Prosperity-focused private sector unions are the solution. That's particularly true for unions serving manufacturing, energy, and heavy industry. Though the union bosses may enjoy sharing a corrupt gravy train with Democratic politicians, progressivism is destroying workers' lives. Once again, Donald Trump began the outreach. An energized restorationist movement must continue it.

It may seem ironic that the "easiest" strategic lessons emerge from the Arab/Israeli conflict, racial justice, and contemporary Islam. It's not. It's deeply instructive. An effective offense requires taking enemy territory. The more comfortable the progressive enemy is in thinking the territory safe—or unnavigable for restorationist forces—the more susceptible it is to penetration.

Others strategic imperatives are harder. They require us to play defense. Defenders don't get to choose their battlefields. Progressivism has won control of our language and our key institutions. If we want to restore America, we'll have to take them back. That means that we must forge and master weapons appropriate for those battlefields: On the battlefield of language, we need linguistic weapons to counter deconstruction, fabrication, and projection. On the battlefield of institutions, we must find ways to alter the incentive structures of academia, the media, and the government.

No one said it was going to be easy.

DEMAND THE TRUTH

Let's start with language. We've already seen that the primary linguistic weapons of progressivism are deconstruction, fabrication, and projection. The weapons we need to counter them are definition, examination, and reflection, respectively.

Deconstruction, recall, is an academic theory that says that words have no fixed meaning. If a progressive hears about something you said, he or she can hold you responsible for whatever meaning progressivism assigns to it. Worse, progressives get to redefine words at will, often inverting their meanings. That lets them, for example, promote racism while parading as antiracists. Progressive deconstruction lets them claim to own every word with positive associations and oppose every word with negative associations. It's a central element in their seduction of decent Americans. It can be devastating.

How do we counter it? Demand definitions. Consistently.

Let's take a concrete example. Suppose you say something like, "Obama was a failed president." No doubt, some progressive will call you a racist. Why? To put you on the defensive—particularly if the conversation takes place with persuadable listeners nearby.

Most of us respond instinctively: "How is that racist? I'm not a racist!"

Have those responses ever worked? Of course not. That's fighting on their ground. You wanted to talk about Obama's failures, and instead you're debating whether or not you're a racist. You already lost. At best, listeners will remember that you said something racist and weaseled out from under it. And those listeners are the prize. Progressives mired so deeply in their own progressivism that they equate criticism of Obama with racism are already lost. There isn't much point in engaging, particularly in public—where they most like to attack. Public debates with progressives are entirely about the third-party onlookers, some of whom may remain persuadable.

Want a better defense? Try asking, "How do you define racist?" Most progressives will start spluttering and say something like, "Everyone knows what racism is." Then you've got them. Because you can say, "Sure. Racism is when you put people in boxes based on their race. Or when you have different rules or standards for different races. That's what the word means. Because I'm opposed to racism, I think we should hold Obama to the same standards we've used for every other president. By those standards, he was a dismal failure. Now, if you think we should use different standards, then you're the racist. So what is it? Was Obama a failure? Or are you a racist?"

Now you've gained the upper hand. They have to start screaming about structural racism or systemic racism or some other phenomenon that's not actual racism as the term has always been understood. They have to expose themselves—as Black Lives Matter did in June 2020 when a supporter asked *Merriam-Webster* to change the dictionary definition of racism. Of course, if you fail to follow up by pinning them down on their redefinition, listeners may fail to recognize the truth. The purpose of definition is to move from defense to offense. Once on offense, never let up until you've won.

A recent application of that counterattack arose the moment the polls closed on the 2020 election. Media progressives immediately announced that "there was no evidence of fraud." Progressive activists ran with that lead. Many conservatives cowered in fear of finding themselves labeled conspiracy theorists merely for noting statistical oddities. Trained restorationists knew how to counter. The definitional question was clear: "What sort of evidence might you accept?" Rather than debating specific rumors—which is what the progressives wanted—this counterquestion landed the conversation at a much more appropriate place. What do fraudulent elections look like? What sort of evidentiary trails do they produce? How does one reason from such evidence to draw a conclusion? Progressives didn't want to discuss any of those things because the answers made it clear that they were hiding the truth. Demanding a definition shifted the conversation from defense to offense.

Try it some time. See if it works. If what the progressives are saying doesn't make any sense (a rather common occurrence), just ask them to define their words. Once people see how wacky progressive definitions are, they'll be able to see through the lies. You may not win the argument—particularly if you think you can persuade an ideological progressive—but you can impede their seduction. Insisting upon definitions is a great way to keep decent people grounded in American ideals, and to slow if not reverse their slide into social progressivism.

Next, fabrication. Fake news. America's mainstream media just makes stuff up to fit their narratives. "Hey!" they say. "There's no way people could have rejected Hillary after they saw how great things were under Obama. You know what? I bet Russia set the whole thing up!" Then they just keep repeating this nonsense they fabricated to make themselves feel better until it becomes conventional wisdom. Now "everyone knows" that Putin rigged the 2016 election. Nonsense. Garbage. Lies. All of it. That's fabrication.

Defending against fabrication is harder than defending against deconstruction. Progressive fabrications worm their way into conventional wisdom so deeply that most people just assume that they're true. Still, there is a defense: examination. Ask for original sources.

Like this: For years we've been hearing that President Trump is divisive and racist. Those are lies. But they're the kind of lies that "everyone knows." How can you get people to reconsider things they already "know" are true? Only by bringing them back to the original source. Try: "You know, I've been hearing that for years. And I've got to tell you, I know plenty of times that Trump has drawn a line between Americans and non-Americans, but I've never once seen him draw lines among different groups of Americans. Now, I'm sure he's said plenty of stuff I've never heard. So, could you point me to a direct quote or transcript where he divides Americans?" They'll never produce one. Progressive reporters report on reporters who reported on something that seemed sort of like something that Trump sort of said that might have been divisive had he actually said it. Progressive fabrications always cite other progressive fabrications for support. They never rely on primary sources, because primary sources won't support them. That's examination.

Finally, projection is the favored weapon of progressive politicians and activists. They're racists, so they call us racist. They brutalize women, so they call us misogynists. Their policies destroy immigrant communities, so they call us anti-immigrant. They ally with Islamists who terrorize Muslims around the world, so they call us anti-Muslim. Obama, Clinton, and Biden sold favors to foreign powers? They accuse Trump of selling favors to foreign powers. They're planning on rolling out authoritarianism? They accuse the GOP of authoritarianism. They rig elections, pad voter rolls, and promote voter fraud? They accuse patriotic Americans of destroying the integrity of American elections. The list goes on and on and on. But you know what? If you pay attention to what progressives accuse Americans and pro-American politicians of doing, you can get a pretty good indication of what progressives are planning to do themselves. That's projection.

How can we defeat progressive projections? Well, since progressive politicians are in charge of projection, let's look at the only American politician who's taken on progressive projections and won. Donald Trump is a jujitsu master. He challenges every projection with a reflection. "Trump colluded with foreign powers," they scream. Trump says: "Democrats collude with foreign powers." Then, when the facts come out, it turns out that they were lying, and he was right. Did he know he was right when he made the claim? Did he know the specifics that turned out to back him up? I have no idea. I'd guess the answer is sometimes, but that's just a guess. What I do know is that Trump gets the projection game. If they're accusing him of colluding with foreign powers, it's a good bet that they've colluded with foreign powers. Progressives are quite predictable. Any time you hear a progressive projection, turn the tables. That's reflection.

Deconstruction. Fabrication. Projection. Lies. Lies. Lies. That's how progressives fight. That's where they've got the advantage. That's how they destroy people. They get to pick the battlefield because they're playing offense. We might prefer to fight elsewhere, but defenders can't be choosers. We have to fight them where they're attacking us—on the field of language. Definition, examination, and reflection can help the truth shine through progressive lies. That's our only real defense against the progressive seduction that's turned so many well-intentioned people into social progressives. More importantly, it's the only way to set the stage for a counterattack— and there are no victories without a solid offense.

ACADEMIC ACCOUNTABILITY

To restore America, we'll have to do more than defend. We'll have to retake our institutions. We must rebuild American academia, American media, and American government in line with the greatest American traditions. We must break the progressive monopoly on these critical institutions to restore the freedom and responsibility necessary for them to flourish. America needs an academy, a press, and a government it can trust. To earn that trust, our leading institutions must behave responsibly. To get them to behave responsibly, we must alter their incentives. That will take time—decades, likely—and it will not be easy.

First, academia. If we want to rebuild America's universities into a source of national pride, we must start by seeing them for what they are: corporations (albeit nonprofit corporations) that develop products and sell services. The only way to get corporations in any industry to change their internal incentive structures is to alter their external incentive structures. In other words, if we want to fix the way that universities operate, we're going to have to change the ways they make their money.

Most universities have two stated purposes, education and research, and one unstated purpose, "campus life" (e.g., dorms, fraternities, social clubs, sports teams). Each of these purposes defines a distinct product line. In theory, student tuition pays for education, grants and contracts pay for research, and mandatory student fees plus donations pay for campus life.

There's no reason these products—and their corresponding revenue sources—should be bundled together. If a single corporation wants to offer all three, that's unobjectionable, but they must remain distinct. That's particularly true when taxpayers guarantee the loans that students use to cover their tuition because we, as a society, have determined that we benefit from having a broadly educated population. A university that forces students to fund campus organizations or faculty research as a precondition for taking classes is taking unfair advantage of students. A university that redirects tuition dollars toward research or campus life is taking unfair advantage of American taxpayers.

Tuition costs, however, are completely out of control. Tuition has risen nearly three and a half times the rate of inflation for forty years! What have the universities been doing with that money? Certainly not improving the quality of education.

How do they justify it? They don't have to. Universities have created a bizarrely overloaded product larded up with countless elements of student life and expensive administrators. They provide tenured faculty with lifetime appointments completely untethered to any value they might confer upon their students or society at large. They operate like small cities, often protecting their jurisdiction against incursions by the police of the real cities that happen to host them. They run multibillion-dollar endowments as hedge funds, don't pay taxes, get the federal government to guarantee the loans students need to pay their exorbitant tuitions, and remain completely unaccountable to their graduates. They're intentionally inefficient organizations operating to make things comfortable for the Credentialed Elite.

We don't need most of those things, and for the most part we don't need what our universities have become. Education may be a necessity, but the "college experience" is a luxury. For those who can afford it, it can be genuinely rewarding. So too, however, can other experiences open to college-age students—including military service, public service, tutoring, interning, and working. The idea that taxpayers subsidize luxury purchases for so many immature, unappreciative kids should be a source of national shame. The debt we saddle them with in return is pure exploitation.

Furthermore, the lack of accountability universities retain toward the students diverts talented students into dead-end fields of study. An honest institution would drive home to all students—consistently and repeatedly—that an engineering class is likely useful training that will pay for itself, while a course in gender studies is a matter of personal interest unlikely to return anything in the way of useful job skills. An accountable institution would guarantee a large part of the student loans taxpayers hand it. That would immediately motivate universities to direct students toward classes and majors likely to help them handle the debt load.

One of the few upsides of pandemic-driven social distancing was the separation of classroom instruction from the campus experience. With modern technology, distance learning (if done well) is an effective way to deliver a great deal of content. (Admittedly, it works better for math and literature than for laboratory chemistry.) If we really want to fix higher education in America, the first two fixes should involve limiting taxpayer-backed tuition assistance to something credibly tied to the cost of educating students, and making universities accountable for the value of the product they market and sell to students. And that's all before we start rethinking the returns we expect on research funding and the way we treat multibillion-dollar endowments.

It's time for a major push to rethink the bargain among the federal government, universities, and students. It's time to put significant conditions on the free money taxpayers guarantee to these anti-American institutions. To remain eligible for government-backed student loans, universities should be required to maintain minimum teaching loads for all teaching faculty, to reduce the number of administrators significantly, and to ensure that a significant number of classes are taught by full-time faculty. Universities should also have to be transparent about the expected monetary value of the courses of study they offer and accountable to their graduates beyond graduation—at least until their student debt is discharged.

Those changes to the way universities secure their revenues and provide their flagship products will render their internal incentive system unsustainable. The wealthiest few may be able to hold on unchanged, but the overwhelming majority will either adapt or die. In the latter case, new entrants will arise to take their place. Only a radical restructuring of American higher education can restore America's universities to the point that they make America proud.

NEWS WE CAN TRUST

Next, the media.

A free country needs a free press. America has one. Social media is an important part of it.

A free country needs a responsible press. America may have a few responsible outlets, but they're the exception. American media, as a whole, is horribly irresponsible. Social media is worse.

A free country needs a trustworthy press. America's doesn't even come close.

That situation is unsustainable. All freedom rests upon responsibility and trust. The Bill of Rights did more than enshrine free speech and a free press as basic human rights; it codified them as twin pillars of a free society. The theory is simple: truth will ring louder than lies, good opinions will defeat bad, and dangerous beliefs will be dispelled faster in public than if kept secret.

That's just a theory. It's easy to cite counterexamples where lies, bad ideas, and dangerous beliefs won the day. Peer pressure, societal norms, powerful voices, and seductive advertisements can convince almost anyone to believe almost anything. Freedom of speech and of the press can only benefit society if a critical mass of speakers—and a critical volume of voices—wield their freedom responsibly. If society motivates its members to seek and value truth, truth will prevail. If not, truth will fade into an afterthought. As it has.

Once again, we did it to ourselves. The incentives shaping today's American press reward manipulation and propaganda rather than responsibility and integrity. In the landmark 1964 case *New York Times v. Sullivan*, the Supreme Court ruled that to win a defamation suit, a public figure must prove that a media outlet acted with "actual malice—that is, with knowledge that [the reported material]

was false or with reckless disregard of whether it was false or not."
While this unshackling of the press has had some positive effects, it
does not work in the service of truth. A reporter who hears a nasty
rumor about a public figure has an incentive to be the first to report
it, not to investigate its truth. In fact, the less the reporter knows, the
better. Investigating a rumor might produce evidence pointing in different directions or suggesting that reality is more complicated than
it seemed. That would burden the reporter. Far better to introduce
every rumor that feeds the prevailing progressive narrative with:
"According to well-placed sources…"

The "actual malice" standard motivates, promotes, and rewards
sensationalistic gossip rather than honest investigative reporting. Not
surprisingly, mainstream American media excels at sensationalistic
gossip. Media outlets get away with it because it's painfully difficult to
prove that intentional ignorance plus casual inattention to the truth
equals actual malice.

The incentives shaping social media are even worse. Section 230
of the Communications Decency Act (CDA) may set a record for
dismal incentives. The CDA is a 1996 law designed to address a specific problem. Early Internet sites permitted any user to post anything. When some conscientious sites began removing pornography,
they found themselves facing defamation suits. The legal theory was
that anyone capable of pulling anything qualifies as a publisher of
everything that remains posted. Section 230 created an exemption
to let people remove harmful material without assuming publisher's
liability. The courts then misinterpreted that exemption as a catch-
all, enabling Internet companies to escape any and all liability for
anything posted on their sites no matter how much editorial control
they retained over the posted material.

Good intentions aside, the CDA ensured that Internet companies have no incentive to curate postings responsibly. To the contrary, their incentive is to cater to their own tastes, whims, and preferences. It's hard to underestimate the danger of motivating giants like Twitter, Facebook, and Google to filter information to suit their own personal, political, or monetary interests. We're suffering through the consequences of those incentives today. The opening weeks of 2021 are likely but a small taste of what's to follow unless we rework the incentives driving social media platform companies.

Taken together, we chose to motivate the progressive press and social media to destroy our freedom. First we told the press to exert only enough effort verifying facts to avoid being found provably malicious. Then we told the social media giants they didn't even have to do that. Every incentive we've handed them has motivated them to shape public discourse to suit their own tastes. Surprise! That's precisely what they've done. Those tastes are progressive? Another shocker.

If we want to fix America's media—including social media—we're going to have to change those incentives. We need to tell the media to get their facts straight before reporting them; a pattern of consistent errors, particularly if they all point in the same direction, should be taken as an indication of ill intent. As to social media? That's easy. Either they're bulletin boards that let people post at will, or they're publishers that curate and arrange those posts. There's plenty of room for both models on the Internet. No one should be permitted to behave like a publisher while escaping the liability we typically assign to publishing misconduct.

The progressive media has a lot in common with progressive academia. They're two industries we've empowered to attract money while preserving zero accountability. The external incentives we've given them undermine the deal at the heart of America: We've handed them tremendous freedom exempt from responsibility. It's hardly shocking that incremental outrageousness has become the key to success in both of these critical industries. If we want to restore their American character, we're going to have to change those regulatory incentives.

REINVENTING GOVERNMENT

Finally, that third pillar of progressive control: the government. There's plenty to say about government reform, but fairly little of it is new. There are, however, three areas worth highlighting: public sector unions, election integrity, and regulatory complexity.

Public sector unions need to go. All of them. Public sector unions, by their very nature, funnel taxpayer money to politicians, with whom they then negotiate to funnel taxpayer money to union bosses. That's corrupt by definition. Progressives love it. Money sent to public sector unions is money in the pockets of progressive politicians and causes.

In addition to lining progressive pockets, public sector unions hold in line any civil servants who might feel inclined to question the conventional wisdom governing Credentialed Elite orthodoxy. Perhaps even more damaging, they protect America's worst civil servants from job discipline and firing. To the extent that America suffers from abusive policing, it's not because of some mythical systemic racism. It's because it's too hard for individual departments to discipline and fire abusive cops. The same is true across government. Malicious clerks at the Social Security Administration may make for less compelling videos than do violent cops, but the harm they cause is just as real.

Eliminating public sector unions would represent two great steps toward the American restoration: it would improve the incentives for civil service excellence, and it would end the corrupt slush fund powering progressive activism.

Next, elections. Election integrity is critical. Progressives never had any intention of participating in a free and fair election in 2020. They announced the mechanisms they planned to use to rig the vote loudly and proudly, then projected the fraud onto President Trump. In truth, the Democrats' 2020 campaign against integrity was many election cycles in the making.

Democrats have long opposed commonsense voter security and voter ID laws—an opposition that makes sense only among those eager to promote fraud. In the absence of ID requirements, they spent years padding voter rolls. In 2012, they weaponized the IRS against opposing grassroots activism. It worked.

In 2016, they purchased favors from foreign powers and deployed federal agencies to spy on and interfere with the Trump campaign. A compliant progressive press jettisoned every last shred of professionalism to become the propaganda arm of the Democratic Party. When even that didn't work, their strategy for the 2020 election left nothing to chance.

The moment the dust settled on the 2016 election, progressives began brainstorming ways to secure one-party rule—no matter what America's voting citizens may want. Their deliberations, which they helpfully broadcast via social media, quickly became parodies of themselves. Prominent Democrats promised to impeach President Trump, for no particular reason, from the day he entered office (if not earlier). Then they delivered, in what can only be called a thinly veiled coup attempt. Then they delivered again as he was on his way out the door. What unprecedented actions had Trump taken to warrant two impeachments? He threatened to expose progressive corruption, first in a phone call, then in a speech.

Since 2016, progressives have also been making noises about—and moving toward—eliminating the electoral college to rework our electoral system; redoing the federalism at the heart of our constitutional structure; giving the vote to noncitizens, felons, and teenagers; and packing the Supreme Court to ensure its blessings of these schemes. All of these threats to transform the structure of American government began long before Justice Ginsburg's death "provoked" Senate minority leader Chuck Schumer to announce that if the Democrats were to regain power, "nothing would be off the table." Why? To save American democracy, of course. If you're a progressive, it's a perfectly sensible deconstruction. After all, the ends justify the means.

The Democrats' 2018 performance—particularly in California, whose ballot harvesting provisions were designed to maximize voter fraud—showed that they were done taking chances. Every close race the GOP led as of election night ended in a Democrat victory when late-arriving harvested ballots were added. Progressives simply won't allow free and fair elections any place they control the levers of state; there are too many deplorable Americans who might vote wrong. What worked in California in 2018 was unrolled nationwide in 2020.

Progressives also like to threaten and attack citizens who refuse to fall in line. In July 2019, San Antonio's Democratic Congressman Joaquin Castro compiled and publicized a list of his own constituents, mostly homemakers and retirees, who had made donations to President Trump. He claimed that his goal was to "shame" them (as if that were an acceptable way for an elected official to treat law-abiding citizens), but it looked more like a hit list of people and businesses to harass, boycott, harm—or worse. Progressives systematically use social media to attack, threaten, and destroy anyone who disagrees with their agenda—with the active encouragement of

Silicon Valley and the media. In early 2021, Silicon Valley moved from its supporting role to a position of leadership in viewpoint suppression and cancellation.

In fact, we know how to run secure elections: promote integrity, not turnout. Close registration well ahead of the election. Check ID. Cross-check signatures. Require paper ballots and in-person, election-day voting. Limit absentee balloting to a small number of legitimate reasons. Require that observers representing all candidates on the ballot be present when votes are counted.

In such an election, everyone who considers voting important will vote. Fraud will be rare. Voting may be a right of citizenship, but citizens who lack the minimal personal responsibility to secure their votes are unlikely to enhance America's governance by voting. Anyone upset because their own irresponsibility once cost them the opportunity to cast a vote will learn an important lesson. That sort of education would make a far greater contribution to American civic engagement than a last-minute, ill-considered vote.

There's no way to restore America without ensuring the integrity of our elections. Which is why it's entirely unsurprising that progressives oppose any measure capable of enhancing election integrity and favor those that enable fraud. With Joe Biden in the White House, things will only get worse. His inauguration ratified the procedures that made the 2020 election such a farce, and progressives will never relinquish them willingly. What works once will be repeated. In fact, we've already seen it repeated; many of the same structural flaws that shattered the credibility of November's presidential election resurfaced in January's Georgia Senate runoffs. An American restoration is impossible until we restore the integrity of our electoral processes. Georgia provided clear evidence that November had not been some anti-Trump exception. The entire system is broken.

Finally, regulatory complexity. Remember the Newly Credentialed progressives who graduated to become complexifiers? Well, nothing in contemporary life is as complex as the Code of Federal Regulations (CFR). The CFR adds so many compliance costs that instead of investing in growth, American businesses invest in protecting themselves from the attacks of entitled bureaucrats, regulators, and lawyers. We motivate those businesses to pull money out of paychecks and raise consumer prices to pay for that compliance.

It's not just the businesses, though. Don't even think about buying a home, a car, or health insurance; securing a mortgage; borrowing money; getting married or divorced; having a child; assisting a parent; inheriting an asset; starting a business; or building, planting, or selling something. Because if you do, you'll have no choice but to hire a Credentialed Elite translator.

The complex regulatory state is the ultimate partnership of big government and big business against hardworking taxpayers, small businesses, families, and individuals. Big government likes big business because an industry with a few big players is far easier to control than an industry with many small ones. Big business doesn't mind ceding a bit of autonomy to a government that works overtime keeping the big guys big and their small competitors small. Oligarchs and oligopolists get along swimmingly.

Compliance costs are a deadweight loss on the economy, but they're a gift to progressives and the Credentialed Elite. They create an abundance of overpaid, unproductive, elite enforcement jobs. They're a protection racket for the big, the rich, and the connected. They're a scam to destroy social mobility. Regulatory complexity is the best mechanism progressives have devised to keep the insiders on the inside and the outsiders on the outside. That's why, no matter the problem, the progressive solution is always increased regulation.

The cost of a regulatory code whose primary purpose is keeping the Credentialed Elite in elite jobs is borne by everyday Americans, who find it hard to get ahead—much harder than it needs to be. The ante for today's America keeps all but the high rollers out of the room. Complexity corrupts the system. Corruption kills trust. Progressivism has elevated complexity-born corruption to an artform.

Here's an engineering tip. You can't improve a complex system by increasing its complexity. Guess what? Guess how we respond to every challenge? Yep. We increase complexity. Every crisis leads to new and more complex regulations designed to increase costs and reduce accountability. Why? Because the goal is rarely to improve the government and serve the citizens. The goal is to increase the government's power, and its discretion, so that progressives can sell favors to their friends.

President Trump introduced a new model when we got hit with a pandemic: he reduced complexity, cut red tape, and engaged the private sector. Those were the best part of any country's response, and the only ones that will confer long-term benefits. So, of course, the progressive elite vilified him for it.

The United States needs a far shorter, far simpler, body of laws and regulations. Decent people should know that decent behavior is legal without having to hire professionals. Decent business owners should invest their money in improving their businesses, serving their customers, and paying their employees—not in ensuring that that they comply with incomprehensible laws and regulations. Decent families should never worry that the government will interfere in family relationships or seize private property for failure to follow some obscure and incomprehensible law.

It's entirely possible to keep our food and water wholesome, our environment clean, our infrastructure secure, our roads and skies safe, our communications effective, our banking and securities exchanges honest, and our tax code fair, in a manner that most Americans can understand. When we achieve those goals, we'll find enormous resources that we can divert from lawyers and lobbyists to the productive parts of our economy and the institutions of civil society. Anyone who wants to play by the rules will win. The only losers will be those who prefer to write their own rules—and the professionals who enable them. In other words, it would be great for the American Ambitious, terrible for the Credentialed Elite.

That's why the regulatory simplification program President Trump launched was so important; it empowered Americans while weakening progressives. It's why the progressive Biden Administration's deep commitment to complexification is so tragic. America needs a massive, widespread, "zero-based" simplification of the entire CFR: We must review every existing regulation (and law) and justify its continued existence based upon current needs. Anything we can't justify is simply funneling compliance costs from the pockets of hard-working Americans and investors to fund the progressive takeover of our country. We can never restore America while our regulatory systems continue to strangle us in complexity.

We've got our work cut out for us—and it's not about to get easier.

6

TWENTY–TWENTY VISION

MADE IN CHINA

In late 2019, the Chinese Communist Party (CCP) unleashed a plague upon the world. Many of the specifics are still unknown. For present purposes, many of them don't much matter. What matters is that a dangerous virus moved from a lab in Wuhan to infect the surrounding population. With the help of the World Health Organization (WHO), the CCP spread misinformation about the communicability of this virus. By the time the world appreciated the threat, we were in the grips of a global pandemic.

In the United States, the progressive cult of expertise sprang into action. The CCP had handed them an incomparable gift. Could there ever be a clearer case for trusting the experts? Top epidemiologists and previously obscure public health officials took to the podium. The progressive cultists dominating the press placed them on a pedestal. The choice was clear: defer to the experts in all things or assume culpability as a mass murderer.

The President's initial instincts had leaned in a very American direction, attempting to preserve maximal liberty while promoting individual responsibility: Limit entry into the country to minimize exposure. Minimize coercion, keep the economy functioning as well as possible, and provide assistance to those hurt most directly by this global pandemic. Prioritize treatment of the most vulnerable populations. Promote increased hygiene and other responsible individual behavior. Galvanize the private sector to take coordinated action. Motivate domestic manufacturing of protective gear and therapeutics. Ensure that health care providers and insurers absorb the bulk of the public costs. Focus on logistics to get portable resources to wherever they're needed most. Eliminate red tape standing between useful innovations and the marketplace. Flow resources to those working on therapies and vaccinations. Streamline regulatory burdens to speed development, testing, and deployment of a vaccine. Announce any positive results with a hopeful spin. Try to keep people optimistic to minimize their panic. Take calculated steps to minimize the number of collateral deaths that would arise were our hospitals overwhelmed with virus patients—that is, "flatten the curve." Understand, however, that such flattening is a matter of deferring infection and death, not of preventing it.

It was a fine plan, reminiscent, in many ways, of FDR's pivot to galvanize American industry upon entry into World War II. It recognized that a free society has certain limitations, and it trusted Americans to behave responsibly. It also recognized that though serious enough to warrant unprecedented actions and expenditures, this Wuhan-born coronavirus was hardly the bubonic plague. We would not lose a quarter of our population—as London had done during twenty-two weeks in 1665. Contact with this virus was hardly a death sentence. Most of the people who came into contact with it would not get infected. Most who became infected would not get sick. Most who got sick would experience relatively mild symptoms. Most with severe symptoms would recover. Only among those who were already weak—elderly, frail, immunocompromised, morbidly obese—was there anything greater than a 1 percent risk of death. Even the experts conceded all those points.

There was no way to escape this pandemic without incurring a significant national cost. Left entirely unchecked, the virus might have killed a few million Americans. Mitigation measures of the sort that would let life function more or less normally for most of the population would have brought that number way down. To those who understand statistical science, the proper approach was obvious: The "80/20 rule" is an empirical observation that it's often possible to gain 80 percent of the benefit of a solution for only 20 percent of the cost; that final 20 percent soaks up most of the expense. President Trump, as a savvy businessman, set out to find the way to gain maximum benefits at minimal costs.

That approach would have been solid, rational, well-founded, and (as noted) characteristically American. It might have worked had it been given a chance. It never got one. Instead, a panicked supermajority handed power to progressive experts. They assumed command through a very important piece of the president's own plan: the task force he assembled to address the pandemic was a Trojan horse. It was stocked with experts who somehow neglected to teach America about the 80/20 rule.

The Credentialed Elite experts on that task force promoted a false choice: On the one hand, science and expertise were working hard to protect American life. On the other, base greed and nefarious political interest were conspiring to sacrifice American lives upon the altar of profit. A responsible media would have reminded the American public that even during a public health crisis, when public health considerations assume a vastly elevated importance, public policy must nevertheless balance multiple concerns. America's progressive media instead insisted that public health experts drawn from the ranks of America's safely progressive bureaucracy should dictate the new shape of American life.

The Credentialed Elite experts in charge also neglected to mention another important point: sometimes, as in the case of this pandemic, the "best available scientific assessment" isn't particularly good. Any decent statistical modeler willing and able to think clearly could tell that the data upon which these experts relied were deeply flawed, rendering their models effectively useless. Reliable data require fixed definitions and consistent reporting mechanisms. In this crisis, particularly in the early going, the data didn't even pretend to have either. In a hallmark of progressive science—and in stark contrast to the actual scientific method—meaningless data input into questionable models to yield speculative conclusions consistent with the desired narrative justified draconian restrictions on human freedom.

The progressive fear campaign worked. The experts scared America into submission. So the experts, in true cult form, locked us in our homes, shattered our communities, kept us from our houses of worship, and destroyed our livelihoods. All for our own good.

It was the clearest, smoothest demonstration of the progressive cult of expertise in action the world has seen to date. The experts empowered the authoritarian instincts the cult had instilled in its progressive political emissaries. Governors, mayors, county officials, and even HOA boards came unfettered. The shackles the Constitution had long placed on their actions came undone.

It was a glorious moment for the Credentialed Elite. They were finally in complete control. They moved immediately to destroy their true enemy, the American Ambitious. They ran roughshod over small business—the primary mechanism allowing traditional, ambitious, hard-working Americans to escape the behemoth of progressive culture. They pummeled minorities and workers to an unprecedented degree, heightening reliance on the government for handouts. But the progressive onslaught was just beginning.

The second wave, launched Memorial Day Weekend, was designed to stoke fear and rage among the Terrified Minorities while crippling the police necessary to preserve American safety and freedom. The notion of structural, or systemic racism leaped to the front pages. Recall, unlike actual racism—which describes attitudes and behavior—structural racism wafts through the ether. Colorblind "white" Americans who see skin color as little more than descriptive, and who have never considered race when making any decision, awoke to discover that they were "racists." Not because they're actually racist, mind you, but because they'd spent their lives trying to navigate the world, earn a living, raise a family, and enjoy a bit of leisure time—all while having been born into a "racist system."

Shockingly, plenty of decent people internalized the defamation and came to think less of themselves. Others accepted the progressive racial divisions and chose to embrace their own. It's hard to think of a better recruiting ad for white supremacism than the scenes of progressive crowds self-segregating into "black people" and "white people." Whether the "white people" were then told to kneel to "black people," wash the feet of "black people," or stay out of safe spaces, the message was clear: Progressives have no interest in eliminating racism. They seek to invert the order of degradation.

Such scenes clarify a point that has long been clear but is rarely stated. White supremacists share the progressive worldview; they simply disagree as to who should emerge on top. In 2014, when progressives first declared their race war in Ferguson, they did it in part to awaken white supremacism. Why? To project. Progressive activists implausibly blame resurgent white supremacism on colorblind Americans rather than on their own racist worldview. The progressive media repeats the defamation often enough to embed it in conventional wisdom.

It's far beyond time for restorationist reflection. White supremacists are a uniquely important part of the progressive universe—the designated villains. In our traditional American world, they are but one evil among many. Like all other evils, they say what they say, praise who they praise, and vote how they vote for their own reasons. They have no place in a restored America. Restorationists loathe white supremacists because they're supremacists; progressives hate them because they're white. Progressives embrace all nonwhite supremacist movements. It's hard to think of anything more anti-American.

THIS WAS AN UPRISING

Progressives insist that the draconian restrictions on freedom and the celebration of rioting are only temporary. They're not. They're a critical component of the progressive transformation, a hallmark of their utopian, postrepublican elitist oligarchy.

Social distancing is merely the logical destination toward which our progressive Credentialed Elite have been taking us for decades.

It's the ultimate form of control. The Credentialed Elite can work remotely, comfortably, and at full pay. Elite members of the American Ambitious can do the same. Everyone else suffers. Everyone else becomes a ward of the state, reliant on government handouts for basic sustenance. The mere act of being outside, congregating to pray, or trying to meet a friend becomes antisocial and dangerous. Progressives will never willingly relinquish the power to differentiate "essential" from "nonessential" activities. In another sign that progressivism is becoming a full-blown faith, progressive missionary work, evangelism, and fear campaigns have become the most essential of all human activities. Even public health was secondary when progressive riots were at stake.

Those demonstrations and riots, in turn, are easily recognizable as regime-change tactics. Ideological progressives have long focused on regime change. Their open advocacy is readily available, but few other than ideological progressives and a handful of us renegades have bothered to read it.

Take, for example, Paul Engler's *Resistance Guide*, published shortly after Donald Trump became president. Engler, who'd called for an uprising even when Barack Obama was in the White House, is the rare and dangerous combination of theorist and activist. As an activist, he launched a "movement incubator" called Momentum in 2014; it has already incubated influential groups pushing radical climate change politics, open borders, and antisemitism. As a theorist, Engler brought forward the work of two significant predecessors: Saul Alinsky and Gene Sharp.

Saul Alinsky, the premiere labor organizer of the mid-twentieth century, is best known for his *Rules for Radicals*. Alinsky was a brilliant organizational theorist who knew the importance of studying yourself and your adversaries to inventory strengths and weaknesses. His rules all flowed from those assessments. They teach large, disorganized groups of people unhappy with the status quo how to leverage collective behavior to change their work and life environments. Alinsky, however, was a midcentury thinker. While his rules remain tactically useful, social and technological changes have rendered many of his observations and strategies dated.

Engler applied lessons from open-source development, networking, and social media to bring Alinsky's work into the twenty-first century. Though Engler doesn't cite those inspirations, these tech-driven advances in organizational thinking give life and power to his activism. Engler advises all resistance members to find "small groups" of friends with whom to share their activism, brainstorm, and provide mutual emotional support. As nice as that sounds, it masks a dark side. These small groups ensure that each activist's entire social and emotional life remains within the movement. Anyone wavering risks having their closest friends become informants and enemies. The proper name for such a group—within both communications and activism—is "cell," a term Engler studiously avoids.

Communication among Engler's activist cells is straightforward. Resistance leaders provide slogans, propaganda, basic talking points, and overarching goals. Individual cells brainstorm and perform as they see fit. Each new cellular initiative gets posted to the network; some go viral while most die quietly. Most information stays local until it's posted, at which point it becomes public. No one is ever privy to the full scope of operations—meaning that no one can ever whistleblow or testify about more than a small piece of a large plan. It's a brilliant contemporary strategy for an organic movement. It's also brutally effective. Consider, for example, its deployment in the 2020 election. Peter Navarro's meticulous review of election irregularities summed it up beautifully: "Theft by a thousand cuts across six dimensions and six battleground states rather than any one single 'silver bullet' election irregularity." That's a sign of an effective cellular network, not of a coordinated conspiracy.

Gene Sharp—a scholar of nonviolent uprisings—distilled and cataloged the lessons of history. He drew a distinction between ideological and strategic nonviolence. The Amish insistence upon turning the other cheek when attacked is ideological. Iconic nonviolent leaders like Gandhi and MLK deployed strategic nonviolence. Sharp makes a compelling case that had they commanded armies capable of defeating their enemies, they would have fought more conventionally. Because they did not, they drew instead upon the assets they did command: large followings and moral suasion. In today's America, progressive assets include academia, the media, Hollywood, Silicon Valley, and the civil service. Taking a cue from Sharp, Engler encourages his activist cells to leverage those assets.

Ideological progressives heard the calls progressive politicians and organizations put forward, devised their own cellular implementations, and broadcast their plans. Social progressives joined as a show of support. Non-progressive professionals and corporations followed the incentives before them to become tacit supporters.

With the call for racial justice, resistance cells erupted across the country. George Floyd's death provided progressives the excuse to roll out a long-planned campaign of allegedly grassroots, allegedly nonviolent resistance. Release of the news was choreographed to foment hatred and violence. A grisly YouTube video showing what appeared to be a murderous cop went viral. Progressive authorities withheld the body cam footage and a tox screen proving that much of Floyd's suffering was self-inflicted. Millions of basically decent social progressives—entirely unaware that anti-American progressive ideologs hellbent on regime change were manipulating their emotions—

flocked to the streets. They provided marvelous cover for dangerous, well-funded Marxist radicals.

For months, the anti-American protests cycled through rampant looting, attacking police, terrorizing citizens, and toppling statues. The razor-thin line separating sculpture from text soon emboldened progressive rioters to burn Bibles. Cowering politicians and social progressives around the country rallied behind the deceptively benign slogan "black lives matter," seemingly oblivious to the actual Black Lives Matter organization orchestrating the carnage. Even a quick glance at its "platform" (displayed prominently on BLM websites from its 2016 introduction until at least March 2020) demonstrates hatred for the nuclear family, colorblindness, Jews, and the American dream.

Social progressives, however, can't be bothered with such minor details. The progressive media assures them that Black Lives Matter is an antiracist movement, so they nod approvingly as they watch "antiracist white people" called upon to degrade themselves in penance to "antiracist black people." Then they write checks to these "antiracist" hatemongers to signal their own virtue.

The progressive media megaphone is central to securing social progressives. Because Americans dislike violence, many of America's most dangerous radicals employ the language of nonviolence. Progressive leaders announced nonviolent demonstrations. Local cells organized a mixture of protests and riots around the approved theme of racial justice. The media dutifully insisted they were "mostly peaceful." Anyone familiar with the resistance literature could recognize the regime-change tactics in play.

COLOR REVOLUTION

A more profoundly dangerous set of tactics unfolded in parallel. Progressive leaders called for increased ballot access. Cells around the country, including some inside state and local governments, answered the call. They produced an electoral system that shifted power from voters (where progressives are weak) to bureaucrats, the media, social media, and the courts (where progressives are strong). The media dutifully saw only noble efforts to promote ballot access during a pandemic. Anyone familiar with resistance literature could recognize the regime-change tactics in play.

The progressive fake news campaigns to sell corrupted elections followed the pattern Obama had used so successfully to sell Obamacare and his Iran deal. No surprise then that they drew heavily upon the work of prominent Obama Administration alumni. Credentialed Elite scholars like Brookings' Norman Eisen and Stanford's Michael McFaul did more than project the Trump Presidency as the threat to American democracy that Obama had actually been. Eisen lauded the "color revolutions" drawn from Sharp's work as a defense against "democratic backsliding." McFaul took to Twitter to chastise those who'd given color revolutions a bad name.

While some color revolutions may indeed have prevented backsliding, the techniques hardly depend upon the "anti-democratic" nature of a regime. Color revolutions disempower anti-progressive leaders and movements independent of the popular support they command. In fact, many advocates of color revolutions argue for their use to depose enormously popular leaders clinging to national traditions (some healthy, some nasty) and install progressive elites. In doing so, of course, they must first deconstruct "nonviolence," "democracy," and "international norms" to claim legitimacy for their favored elites.

The hallmark of a color revolution is an election restricted to one "legitimate" outcome. Staged protests challenging the moral legitimacy of an existing regime are common in the lead-up to the vote. So too are altered election rules claiming to expand ballot access and control ballot counting. Perhaps above all, propaganda is key. Typical reports might trumpet opposition popularity and contempt for the regime, amplify opposition narratives, deride the views of regime supporters, or predict an easy opposition victory. The obvious corollary is that if the regime claims victory, it must have cheated. In other words, color revolutions deploy "elections" in which any outcome other than the preferred one would lack moral and legal legitimacy. Such an election lacks credibility. It cannot reasonably be considered free and fair even if the preordained outcome happens to reflect the true will of the citizens.

Many advocates of color revolution techniques are more-or-less ambivalent about the true will of the citizens. Genuine popular support may make their task easier, but it's hardly necessary. The techniques can work equally well with truth, gross exaggeration, or outright fabrication. They can install a legitimately popular opposition or merely an opposition with powerful patrons. Either way, their purpose is to ensure that the pre-selected progressive (or at the very least, progressive-friendly) candidate emerges with control of the national government.

Prior to the 2020 election, a few brave sources tried to ring the alarm about America's pending color revolution. They deserved far more attention than they received. Many common elements of color revolutions appeared in America for the first time in 2020.

The latter half of 2020 featured a new twist on fake news: outright suppression. In the weeks and months leading into the election, the progressive media refused to ask Joe Biden any meaningful questions about anything. It suppressed hard news about Biden family corruption and its ties to the CCP. It wrote off progressive street violence and fabricated a threat from white supremacists. It lied about the pandemic, the shutdowns, the economy, and President Trump's handling of the crisis. It derided numerous accurate statements from Trump and his supporters as self-evidently false while endorsing outright lies by and in support of Biden. Meanwhile, progressive politicians and activists launched a campaign to flood the country with unsupervised ballots in a manner that enabled massive electoral fraud. So of course progressives accused President Trump and his supporters of suppression and fraud.

In November, having changed numerous rules surrounding the administration of the election with minimal notice and dubious authority, progressive bureaucrats and activists dispensed with the procedures typically used to verify and validate returned ballots. Amid numerous irregularities surrounding the supervision and tabulation of ballots, progressives reported election results incompatible with historical patterns, statistical expectations, and political logic. So of course progressives accused President Trump and his supporters of violating democratic norms and "threatening our democracy."

Meanwhile, the tactical street riots and violence disappeared the moment progressive forces claimed the mantle of legitimacy for Joe Biden. They'll remain largely out of sight until progressives once again find them useful. So of course progressives accused anyone suggesting that Democrats deployed tactical violence of spouting conspiracy theories.

Before the vote tallies were complete, progressive media and social media proclaimed that "there was no evidence of fraud." Few restorationists were well enough trained in definition to demand to know what such evidence might look like or how it might have been produced so quickly. So of course progressives labeled as fraudulent any suggestion that the reported results lacked credibility.

As testimonial, video, statistical, and forensic computing evidence mounted, progressives equated technical legal constraints with reality. As a matter of law, if nothing requires a state to clean its voter rolls before mass-mailing unrequested ballots, the mass mailing is legal. If nothing prohibits third parties from administering, collecting, and handling massive numbers of ballots, those actions are legal. If a state conducts a legal election, the law presumes that the reported results are valid, and places the burden on anyone challenging them to prove otherwise. Anyone proffering such proof must compile a complex factual record in a matter of weeks. (By way of comparison, Robert Mueller had over two years, a sizable team, and an unlimited budget to review the 2016 election.)

With those legal standards in place, the rest was easy. The progressive media used every unsubstantiated rumor, every dead-end inquiry, and every gap in witness credibility to discredit the growing body of substantiated evidence. They portrayed every denial of wrongdoing as evidence of virtue. Most importantly, they equated technical court rulings with facts.

The focus on legality is a sleight of hand that was relevant only until the inauguration. The far more important question concerns the credibility of electoral procedures. That analysis is completely factual. It hinges entirely on the nature of the procedures. Legality is irrelevant. Presumptions are misplaced. Common sense suggests that when every detected irregularity and anomaly favors the side that had been most adamant about changing rules, reducing security, and mass-mailing ballots, the election was rigged before the first votes were cast. Fortunately for progressives, the Credentialed Elite require everyone entering American higher education to dispense with common sense in favor of deference to the experts.

The entire 2020 election was an exercise in projection. Anyone willing to apply common sense could see that America's progressive elite mobilized to rig it. The tragedy is that some of their most insidious steps toward the preordained outcome were legal. Timelines, complexity, and evidentiary standards precluded meaningful remedies for the illegalities. Nothing about the process was trustworthy. So of course, progressives enshrined the defamation that those calling out the election's obscenities weakened faith in America's institutions.

America's institutions are deeply unworthy. While some brave restorationists countered with reflection, no American institution stood with them. Most ominously, when Texas sued Pennsylvania and twenty-plus states joined each side, the Supreme Court abdicated its role as arbiter. If anyone needed a harbinger of future instability, that was it. A house divided against itself is least likely to stand when its factions lose faith in the mechanisms of peaceful conflict resolution. Where conflict abounds and nonviolent resolution is unavailable, violence will flare. Mobs and warlords will replace elections and judges. The Credentialed Elites and corrupt institutions that render such violence rational are culpable for all that follows.

The 2020 election illustrates how progressivism has brought Alinsky and Sharp forward. Progressives inventoried their strengths and chose their battlefields wisely. They moved the selection of America's president from the citizenry to the bureaucracy. After all, why take chances with a deplorable bunch of reactionary, violent, superstitious bigots? Color revolutions are the province of bureaucrats, intelligence operatives, and the press. Progressive Credentialed Elites dominate all of those areas.

They were hardly subtle about it, either. Amidst the countless, breathless warnings from our elite that only radical conspiracy theorists questioned the integrity of the election, *Time* magazine published what it called "the inside story of the conspiracy to save the 2020 election." In keeping once again with the patterns of color revolution, the self-described conspirators took enormous pride in their efforts, casting themselves as saviors: "they were not rigging the election; they were fortifying it."[*]

In fact, the operatives behind this "fortification" were eager to tell their story, "even though it sounds like a paranoid fever dream—a well-funded cabal of powerful people, ranging across industries and ideologies, working together behind the scenes to influence perceptions, change rules and laws, steer media coverage and control the flow of information." They proudly "touched every aspect of the election. They got states to change voting systems and laws and helped secure hundreds of millions in public and private funding. They fended off voter-suppression lawsuits, recruited armies of poll workers and got millions of people to vote by mail for the first time. They successfully pressured social media companies to take a harder line against disinformation . . ."[†]

Those are precisely the sorts of efforts students of Alinsky and Sharp would undertake, and precisely the way they'd proclaim their own heroism. A discerning observer might note that despite touching "every aspect of the election," they exerted no apparent efforts to ensure that voter rolls were clean and accurate, secure the mailed ballots that spent weeks circulating freely, verify the legality

---

[*] Ball, Molly. "The Secret Bipartisan Campaign That Saved the 2020 Election." *Time*, 4 Feb. 2021. http://www.time.com/5936036/secret-2020-election-campaign/.

[†] *Ibid.*

of individual ballots, ensure functional oversight of vote-counting, or maintain auditable information. In other words, their involvement touched upon every aspect of the election other than those capable of ensuring ballot integrity.

With Joe Biden now ensconced in the White House, the key question is no longer whether he got there legally. The law presumes that he did, no authorized institution has overridden that presumption, and there is no way to remove the legality of his inauguration retroactively. Nor is the question whether America's eligible voters truly cast the votes that put him there. There's plenty of evidence suggesting they did not, but the data are so corrupt we can never be certain. No, the burning question is whether the electoral system in which Biden declared victory is consistent with a republican form of government. Answer: it isn't. When the Supreme Court refused to protect that constitutional guarantee, the last elite American institution crumbled. Should anyone ever ask what American restorationists most want to restore, the answer is now clear: the American republic.

EXPERTS, EXPERTS ÜBER ALLES

For those who wanted a preview of the progressive utopia, 2020 provided it. Authoritarians at the local level drew lines dividing activities of which they approve from those of which they disapprove. Those who pursue approved activities are exempt from scrutiny, legal action, and the most basic requirements of common decency. Those who simply wish to live their lives risk penalties every time they leave their homes.

Marvel at the demonstration of true progressive power. Yes, the decidedly pro-American, antiprogressive Donald Trump was in the White House, and the GOP held a narrow Senate majority. Yes, the president had the right instincts. None of it mattered. The progressive media invented terrifying fake news: we are all on the cusp of death! As that wore thin: mere existence in our society is racist! Finally: concerns about election integrity are anti-democratic!

We plunged into social distancing without thought, without debate, and without much awareness. The progressive cult of expertise transformed America overnight. In furtherance of its emergence as a full-blown religion, progressivism adopted a sacred garment: the face mask. Though the excuse was medical, the symbolism is ideal. The individual progressive is a faceless representative of an identity group, a nameless cog in the intersectional struggle for social justice.

Progressives had spent decades laying the groundwork; it was just a matter of finding the right excuse. Social distancing is not only a brutally effective form of control. It's the necessary and logical consequence of two defining features of our time: extreme risk aversion and atomization. We embarked down those paths—willingly if thoughtlessly—decades ago. Why? At the behest of experts, of course.

Our risk aversion had become manifest. We'd raised two generations of helicoptered eggshell children. Playgrounds and schoolyards required multiple referees. A hurt child proved that someone had been negligent. Bullying became a form of felonious assault. Teasing was inherently sexist, racist, ableist, or some other form of hate speech tied to long-term psychological damage, oppression, and eventually genocide. The only thing that mattered was the child's self-actualization—whatever that might mean.

We then sent these mollycoddled snowflakes for progressive indoctrination, where they became highly attuned to the slightest offense. Even a microaggression could send them into a hyperventilating tailspin. They arrived on campus so committed to the inalienable right not to be offended that they cowered in the face of even the most mildly provocative idea. They campaigned for blindingly racist segregated safe spaces in which peers sharing superficial characteristics could find shelter from those who resembled their great-grandparents' oppressors (or more accurately, those who resembled the oppressors in some stylized retelling of their ancestral histories). They created environments in which women who owned their sexuality were far too fragile to express it consensually without written contracts.

They graduated into a waiting universe of litigation in which every success story masks tales of exploitation, every producer bears unlimited liability, and every negative outcome can be pinned upon some distant party with deep pockets. They learned to shun any personal responsibility to family, community, or nation, swearing fealty only to the world at large—shattering the American deal linking responsibility to freedom. Instead, they expect some amorphous paternalistic government to bail them out of all difficulties and to ensure that no matter the decisions they might make personally, a generous safety net would catch them.

Perhaps nothing encapsulated this modern ethos better than an ad for Barack Obama's 2012 reelection campaign: "The Life of Julia" told the tale of woman who—from cradle to grave—had neither connections nor concerns. Shorn of familial and communal encumbrances, Julia lived a fine, secure, and apparently fulfilling life thanks to the benevolence of the federal government. The very progressive Julia lived in a world of rarefied risk aversion. No one and nothing could derail her as she moved through life freed of the petty prejudices, concerns, and relationships that had weighed down so many of her ancestors. She lived a wonderfully safe life, free to accomplish anything—have a child (apparently on her own), start a business, even retire to volunteer at a community garden. All that the enlightened, progressive Credentialed Elite asked in return was her compliance with whatever moral judgments they deemed necessary for the advancement of society.

As the Greatest Generation gave way to boomers, Gen Xers, and millennials, an enlightened understanding of history's greatest problems had come into view: earlier generations had taken grave risks in the name of tribe, nation, or God. This monomaniacal focus on survival was inherently supremacist, resting upon the presumption that one's own tribe, nation, or God deserved to survive while others fell. Modern enlightened minds grasped the wisdom of jettisoning such parochial pride to embrace the narcissist that lurks within us all: play it safe, lay low, avoid offense, shun entanglements, and inhabit a cocoon customized to your personal quirks and tastes.

That last point dovetailed brilliantly with technological innovation. A century ago, people spent their evenings socializing with neighbors. The minute schools let out, kids owned the streets. Everyone identified with a faith community, whether or not they possessed personal faith. Cities and neighborhoods boasted of local heroes. People felt a kinship for extended families, neighbors, coreligionists, and coworkers. They counted on all of those people to share their fidelity to God and country. There was nothing new about any of that; it had been true in one form or another since the dawn of time.

Then we learned how to innovate. First came radio, then broadcast television, then cable, then the Internet, then social media. Coupled with headphones and virtual reality goggles, we could customize our entertainment experiences and our media exposure. We could create atomized cocoons perfectly suited to the times. Nothing remotely offensive or provocative could ever intrude. The annoyances inherent in human interaction faded into the background. The wisdom of Jean-Paul Sartre reigned supreme: *l'enfer c'est les autres.*

It was only within that context that the sudden imposition of social distancing could engulf us. We had equipped our lives and our homes to make it possible. Teleworking and distance learning were already recognized phenomena. They let us—or at the very least, a critical mass of our elite—pretend that the gross imposition was but a minor annoyance. Our risk aversion made us more than receptive. Ignore all considerations other than public health? Combat the virus no matter the costs? Sacrifice all in the name of saving lives? Of course! It would be inhuman to suggest otherwise.

Unprecedented policies gained precedent. Fringe ideas entered mainstream consideration. Unthinkable ideas became debatable. Bail out entire industries? Send checks to every American? Give the government equity stakes in privately held companies? Socialize health care? Deny innovators profits on the fruits of their labors? Dispense with religious services? Prohibit social gatherings? Cancel major sports seasons? Empty the prisons? Cease arresting criminals? Penalize businesses for operating? Nationalize key industries? Fine people for failing to mask themselves while minding their own business? Anything and everything was suddenly on the table.

The most massive government overreach in American history happened without any real debate—other than perhaps from those who thought that it was not quite massive enough. The experts told us to stay at home, shun our neighbors, set aside our livelihoods, and avoid communing with God. Like good little sheep, we complied. The streets of New York emptied as its governor increased the danger to—and death rate among—its most vulnerable citizens, then took a victory lap for having done so. The relative few who ventured forth in those early days did so sporting face masks and gloves, stifling the urge to help the elderly navigate supermarket aisles, freezing with terror as children scampered by, glaring with contempt with those whose behavior reflected the faintly remembered ethos of 2019.

In free, developed countries around the globe, governments claimed powers no one had ever granted them. They announced mass quarantines of the healthy and shuttered businesses. They created an environment that eliminated the sources of many people's revenues but kept in place the forces under which their bills would come due. They devastated savings that had taken lifetimes to compile. They shuttered the churches and synagogues to which we might normally flock in times of crisis. For the first time in recent memory, they made us wary of our neighbors in troubling times. "We are all in this together," they announced, while doing everything possible to keep us isolated.

We acquiesced, of course. To do otherwise would have been dangerously antisocial—to risk the health and well-being of the most vulnerable among us. Who would be heartless enough to do that? Other, of course, than the progressive governors who shipped the virus into nursing homes to infect those at highest risk of death. Then again, progressives are always willing to sacrifice a few individuals in the name of the cause. If inflating death tolls scared people into submission, who better to kill off than the most vulnerable?

Overnight, we developed an entirely new morality, coincidentally suited to the needs of the Credentialed Elite. Our most virtuous citizens became those who sit in comfortable homes, busily teleworking, drawing full salaries, and announcing proudly that they'll persist as long as it takes to ensure our safety. It's a morality as old as human history: trust elite leaders to determine what is necessary to serve the public good. Failure to comply—or even willingness to question— marks you as an enemy of the public. It's the morality that America was founded to challenge.

The instant, expert-driven, progressive transformation of American life inflicted immediate, severe, and likely irreparable damage on the country. Worse, it provided progressives with an excellent dry run. Experts had assessed the situation, asserted that our behavior had to be restricted both for our own good and the common good, then turned citizens against each other to ensure compliance. A disturbing number of Americans cheered the authoritarian excesses.

Authoritarianism in the name of public safety is a tried-and-true formula for ending freedom. It's the opposite of America's founding ideals. The American republic was born to prove to the world that individuals freed to make their own choices, permitted to reap the benefits of their victories, and empowered to learn the lessons of their defeats, could create a society that put to shame the best efforts of Europe's kings and nobles, popes and prelates.

That American idea changed the world for the better, but it's been challenged bitterly since day one. Freedom has fallen many times and in many places—invariably using the formula we've seen deployed as experts protect us from a viral pandemic. There's now precedent for its repeated use within the United States. The scariest thing about it is neither the pandemic nor the economic shutdown. The true source of horror is the ease with which a majority of Americans were willing to embrace the reasoning that every one of history's dictators has forwarded to justify the death of freedom. It's hardly surprising that the first event allowed to break through the shutdown was a series of demonstrations, protests, and riots determined to bring down the old order. Nor is it surprising that an apparent color revolution followed shortly thereafter.

Social distancing ushered in the era of elite control. In this brave, new, expert-driven world, the government will provide us with customized cocoons in which an isolated life seems almost bearable. Human contact will dwindle. Life will lose much of its meaning. Nihilism will reign. The anomie epidemic will dwarf all viral epidemics. Suicides, mass shootings, and drug addiction will skyrocket. Domestic abuse and divorce rates will rise. Marriage and birth rates will plummet. The mere act of congregating will become subversive. Religious communities will go underground.

Stunningly, there's nothing much new there. All of those trends were evident long before most Americans ever heard of Wuhan, wet markets, or bat soup. They began when our deep commitment to rational thought and science could find no clear reason to value community, connectedness, or spirituality. That these all seem to be deep human needs was irrelevant; needs that can be neither understood nor explained are easily devalued.

Americans raised with shallow connections to family, faith, nation, and tradition have spent decades wandering through the spiritual wilderness searching for personal meaning. Having already dispensed with every mechanism ever devised to instill meaning in life, American society was well prepared to take its next step toward nihilism. We've been hurtling toward social distancing for quite some time. Now that we've reached it, we like to pretend that it's temporary.

Those of us who seek meaning and connection, community and spirit, individual freedom and personal responsibility, have already lost. The sole remaining question is whether we're willing to fight to restore our lives, our freedom, our country. Otherwise, we can all get used to life in the progressive hellhole to which the cult of expertise has consigned us. Might as well try to enjoy it.

TOO SOON

There's no way to sugarcoat it. The fabric of society collapsed in March 2020 when the world's governments declared a public health emergency and dispensed with the rule of law. Our greatest technologies let our elites enslave humanity while empowering and enriching themselves. We've seen it before. The debasement of industrial-age science and technology brought the worst depravations of World War II. The debasement of information-age science and technology may drag humanity even lower.

The free fall is already underway. Human freedom evaporated in 2020. Incremental outrageousness unleashed inner authoritarians around the once-free world. Horrifying scenes abounded. Citizens of once proudly free countries were fined, arrested, and vilified for engaging in normal commerce, associating with friends, attending religious services, or appearing in public unmasked.

Public health became the catch-all excuse for draconian executive action. Across the US, governors divided human activity into "essential" and "nonessential," then applied different rules to the two categories. States and cities claimed license to attack religion, shutter schools, render workers unemployed, bankrupt communities, eviscerate the credibility of our elections, and harass, arrest, and fine Americans doing little more than minding their own business—all in the name of public health.

None of these emergency measures went through the proper legislative process. Nor did they go through the notice-and-comment period that's supposed to justify our regulations. They arose at the whim of executive officials claiming the right to rule by fiat during an emergency. The people they harmed had little recourse beyond the courts—which were closed for much of the year. Judicial intervention at its very best, however, is a mechanism for correcting past wrongs. Had the constitutional structure that's supposed to restrain governmental attacks on American citizens not failed so spectacularly, we wouldn't have needed judicial remedies.

Freedom couldn't have fallen this far this fast had it rested upon a sound foundation. Perhaps more than anything else, 2020 highlighted how successfully progressivism has eroded the infrastructure of freedom throughout what was once called the free world. The collapse of the grand American experiment into an apparent color revolution put a fitting capstone on a dreadful year. The founding of the American republic marked history's greatest stride forward in the cause of human freedom. Its collapse may come to mark freedom's greatest stride backward.

Joe Biden's inauguration heralded a transformed, postrepublican United States. Its contours are already clear. Its progressive leaders promise a soft form of the Chinese model. An enlightened elite oligarchy will broadcast a new, fluid morality that none may question. Many of those who fall in line will be allowed to prosper in ways that serve the oligarchy's conception of the public interest. Many others will be put on the dole—in exchange for embracing authorized morality and expressing gratitude for government largesse. Citizens will inform on each other to curry favor with local oligarchs. How will progressivism effect these outrages? Incrementally. The American people will comply with each downward step because the incentives governing modern life make silent (if not blind) compliance rational.

The Credentialed Elite will rule as never before. Their Orwellian penchant for deconstruction will serve the new order well. So too will their demonstrated skill at indoctrination. Fake news media and the titans of social media will leverage modern information technology to fabricate and suppress as needed to fit the narrative. Progressive activists and politicians will project their outrages on anyone daring to voice opposition, no matter how tepid. Riches, rewards, and prestige will flow to those most adept at the incremental outrageousness needed to impel the venture forward.

The notions of freedom that have loomed large since the end of World War II have evaporated. The hallmark of that era had been the global export of the ideals of the American founding. Even America's greatest enemies conceded the dominance of those ideals: Authoritarians staged elections to establish their legitimacy. Communists insisted that their totalitarian states were "democratic people's republics."

The erosion of the ideals of freedom began when Barack Obama entered office vowing a progressive transformation. He toured the globe, ashamed of American exceptionalism, apologizing for America's past arrogance and missteps. Authoritarians took note. During the eight years of his maladministration, China, Russia, Iran, Turkey, the Muslim Brotherhood, and the Bolivarians surged forward. They developed tacit and explicit alliances with America's progressives.

Donald Trump's reassertion of American ideals and interests—for the first time since the end of the Cold War—drove those alliances deeper. John Kerry told Iran how to counter the Trump Administration's Middle East policies. China enriched the Biden family. The *Washington Post* beatified Muslim Brotherhood apologist Jamal Khashoggi. Progressive activists and NGOs propped up the PLO. Congressional Democrats railed against antiauthoritarian anti-corruption efforts in Ukraine. Open border activists pushed the agendas of Castro and Maduro. Authoritarians around the world worked with American progressives to undermine President Trump.

These foreign friends of American progressivism all cheered Trump's fall; some appear to have provided actual assistance. They stand poised to reap their rewards. The loosening of pressure on China and Iran are central to Joe Biden's foreign policy agenda. As he helps those countries grow stronger, he will make the elite, progressive, postrepublican America complicit in their crimes. The transformed America will lose its moral standing as a beacon of freedom. American restorationism is about more than just America.

American restoration is about the cause of human freedom.

The challenge is daunting. Miseducated citizens responding as they've been trained to respond will dispense with common sense, fail to ask obvious questions, trust the experts, and comply with each incremental outrage. The progressives now in power have vowed to restructure the country in ways that entrench their transformation. To prevail without bloodshed, we restorationists will have to persuade an American supermajority to oppose progressivism. Supermajorities are hard to build and difficult to sustain. Each faction is prickly and sensitive in its own way. Compromise is always difficult; winners and losers alike are often lacking in grace.

Building a sustainable supermajority means helping social progressives appreciate the freedom and rights they've relinquished in exchange for belonging to the progressive crowd. It means helping minorities recognize that progressive elites have been playing them for suckers, ripping away the American dream just when it was fully within their grasp. It means pursuing policies that may dismay some of the conservatives who failed to conserve America's institutions. It means accepting those who work within the oligarchy to slow the transformation as allies pursuing ineffective tactics, not as enemies. It means remaining awake and clear as society becomes increasingly woke and insane. It means convincing miseducated Americans to reject incremental outrageousness and restore common sense. It may start with an exposé of higher education and its insidious incentive system, but it must march through the institutions. Only then can we decisively defeat progressivism. Only then can we restore America.

The republican spirit cannot prevail against the elite unless the nonelite supermajority can remain united. Uniting them behind the restorationist cause is the challenge of the day. In the meantime, the American nation faces deep existential questions. Will human freedom soon recover from the horrors of 2020? Will the progressive transformation take root? Will we restore the American republic? Is the United States experiencing a revolution or a civil war?

As the newly emboldened Chinese might say, it's too soon to tell.

ACKNOWLEDGMENTS

Far too many people to name helped shape my understanding of the stories in this book, in large part because I've wanted to tell them for a very long time. It is my children, however, who've pushed me to rethink almost everything I know from first principles and make my message accessible to those outside the Credentialed Elite.

That said, I would be remiss if I failed to single out two friends whose input has been instrumental. I met Joe Bernstein during freshman orientation. We quickly discovered a shared passion for understanding pretty much everything. Over the course of forty years we've discussed precisely that, often loudly, on long walks around the progressive enclaves of urban America. We've disagreed as often as we've agreed, but it's never caused either of us to hold back. That's becoming far too rare in today's America, and I appreciate Joe all the more for it.

Several years ago, Jeff Ballabon brought me in to consult on a project that had nothing to do with politics or policy. Turns out, we'd gone to high school together many years earlier, then given each other no thought while taking drastically different life paths to reach many of the same conclusions. Since then, he's become a close friend, confidant, teacher, business partner, and coauthor. If there's a political question, policy debate, or philosophical dilemma that's been in the news in recent years, Jeff is the guy with whom I've hashed it out.

Jeff is also a colleague at the American Restoration Institute (ARI), one of two nonprofits that have allowed me to develop this book's themes. The other is the American Center for Education and Knowledge (ACEK), where Robert Chernin, Jay Shepard, and Ari Storch have provided helpful feedback and support. My opinions and expressions, however, remain strictly my own. They may or may not reflect the beliefs of any other individual or organization.

Finally, Seb Gorka was generous enough to provide encouragement, support, and the book's foreword. Fred Siegel, Harmeet Dhillon, and Joel Pollak provided my earliest reviews. My publishers, Naren Aryal and Michelle Meredith, gave this book its style, shape, title, cover artwork, and exquisite timing—enabling me to release *The New Civil War* just as more and more Americans have come to believe that a new civil war is precisely what we face.

OTHER BOOKS
BY BRUCE ABRAMSON:

American Restoration: Winning America's Second Civil War (American Restoration Institute, 2019).

An American Vision for the Middle East (with Introductions by Jeff Ballabon and Herbert London) (Kindle, 2017).

The Secret Circuit: The Little-Known Court Where the Rules of the Information Age Unfold (Rowman & Littlefield, 2007).

Digital Phoenix: Why the Information Economy Collapsed and How it Will Rise Again (MIT Press, 2005).